JAN   2016

**Designing
Engineering
Solutions**

Inventors of Everyday Technology

Heather S. Morrison

New York

Published in 2016 by Cavendish Square Publishing, LLC
243 5th Avenue, Suite 136, New York, NY 10016

Library of Congress Cataloging-in-Publication Data

Morrison, Heather S., author.
Inventors of everyday technology / Heather S. Morrison.
pages cm. — (Designing engineering solutions)
Includes bibliographical references and index.
ISBN 978-1-50260-660-0 (hardcover) ISBN 978-1-50260-661-7 (ebook)
1. Inventors—Biography—Juvenile literature. 2. Inventions—History—Juvenile literature. I. Title.

T39.M67 2016
609.2—dc23

2015001422

The author would like to thank the following contributors: Laura Lambert, Paul Schellinger, Mary Sisson, Chris Woodford

Editorial Director: David McNamara
Editor: Kristen Susienka
Copy Editor: Michele Suchomel-Casey
Art Director: Jeffrey Talbot
Designer: Alan Sliwinski
Senior Production Manager: Jennifer Ryder-Talbot
Production Editor: Renni Johnson
Photo Research: J8 Media

Contents

Introduction to Everyday Technology

Homes are full of inventions that make them comfortable, efficient, and relaxing. Everything in the home—from chairs and tables to lawn mowers and air-conditioning—was invented by a person who had a vision on how to improve lifestyle. Some inventions made cleaning houses easier, while others were created purely to entertain people living in the home. Regardless, household inventions have become commonplace and continue to improve living for many people around the world.

Most household inventions are relatively recent, dating from the late nineteenth or early twentieth century. The reason is simple: many of them depend upon electricity, which became popular only after Thomas Edison (1847–1931) developed the first power plants in the 1880s. Edison did not know that modern homes would become so reliant on electricity. His objective was simply to sell the idea of electric-powered lighting. Intentional or not, the development of electric power was a milestone in the history of the household that made possible all kinds of labor-saving appliances, making it easier for people to spend more time with their families or on leisure pursuits.

The Advent of Heating and Cooling Systems

Fire was one of the first human inventions, dating back at least a million years. No one knows who invented it or how, but its uses are clear: to provide warmth, safety, and a means of cooking food. Fire, in one form or another, has maintained a steady presence in the home ever since. In Roman times (circa 27 BCE–395 CE), some homes were heated by hot air produced by an underground fire and channeled between the walls and floors using an ingenious network of brick-lined **ducts**. Called a hypocaust, which means "heated from below," it was the earliest example of central heating.

Prior to modern times, many people relied on fires for warmth in cold months.

Until the mid-eighteenth century, most people heated their homes using large open fireplaces. In 1740, the famous American journalist, politician, and inventor Benjamin Franklin (1706–1790) developed what became known as the Franklin stove. This was a large, freestanding iron basket into which wood or other fuel could be loaded. Air could be drawn through the stove freely, thus burning the fuel more effectively and giving off less smoke and more heat. Walter Hunt (1796–1859) was another American inventor who developed a household stove, although he is best known for inventing the safety pin.

English physicist Benjamin Thompson (1753–1814), one of Benjamin Franklin's contemporaries, gained notoriety for his scientific studies of heat. Thompson was one of the first to show that heat is a form of energy. He made his scientific discoveries practical with a number of inventions that improved home heating and cooking, such as a water boiler, a kitchen range, and an improved fireplace.

Inventions that cool homes were also developed through a mixture of trial and error and scientific discovery. One of the simplest home-cooling devices, the electric desk fan, was invented in the 1880s by American scientist Schuyler Wheeler (1860–1923), just four years after Edison's first power plant opened in Manhattan. Most fans move the air around—they do not actually remove any heat—and so the cooling they provide is sometimes an illusion. Air-conditioning, a much-improved way of cooling a building using scientific principles, was pioneered in the first half of the twentieth century by American engineer Willis Haviland Carrier (1876–1950). His systems used special cooling fluids called coolants to soak up the heat in a room and transfer it outside.

Kitchen Aids

The kitchen is the hub of many homes, a place where people cook, eat, and coordinate domestic chores. Food arrives in the kitchen from grocery stores, sometimes carried in the flat-bottomed paper bags that became popular after Margaret Knight (1838–1914) invented a machine for making them in the 1860s. Once in the kitchen, food needs to be kept fresh. Most kitchens have airtight plastic containers for preserving a variety of foods. These were developed in the mid-twentieth century by American inventor Earl Tupper (1907–1983). Cellophane (a thin, clear plastic film) is another way of keeping food fresh. It was invented accidentally by Swiss scientist Jacques Brandenberger (1872–1954), who was trying to devise a chemical coating that would keep tablecloths clean. The plastic he invented turned out to be more useful for preserving food by keeping air away from it.

Most modern kitchens have refrigerators and freezers to store fresh and frozen food. Refrigerators use coolants that circulate to remove excess heat, thus preserving the food inside. The coolants, made from chemicals known as chlorofluorocarbons (CFCs), were developed in 1928 by American chemist Thomas Midgley (1889–1944) and first used in refrigerators made by the Frigidaire Company. However, CFCs were largely phased out in the 1990s after scientists found they caused a hole in the ozone layer, an important part of Earth's atmosphere.

Home freezing is possible not just because of the invention of refrigerators and coolants, but also because American inventor Clarence Birdseye (1886–1956) found a way of "flash freezing" food (cooling it very quickly) in a factory setting. Before frozen food became popular, people had to rely on other methods of preservation. One of the most popular was to seal food in cans, an idea invented in 1810 by French chef Nicolas-François Appert (ca. 1750–1841). Various methods of preserving meat, spices, and oils were also developed by African American inventor Lloyd Hall (1894–1971).

Kitchens contain many of a home's electrical appliances besides the refrigerator—and most of them save huge amounts of time and energy. One appliance often stored in the kitchen is a vacuum cleaner, an invention originally developed by a British engineer in 1901. Until the 1980s, virtually every vacuum caught the dust it collected in a cloth or paper bag, which tended to reduce the cleaner's effectiveness as it filled up. In the 1980s, another British engineer, James Dyson (1947–), began working on a method of vacuuming without the dust bag so a vacuum cleaner would always maintain maximum suction. Dyson's bagless vacuum was successfully launched in the United States in 2002.

Another popular kitchen appliance, the dishwasher, was invented in 1886 by Josephine Cochran (1839–1913). The first automatic dishwashers were entirely mechanical: plates, glasses, cutlery, and other items to be washed were loaded into metal baskets and blasted with hot soapy water to get them clean. Modern dishwashers, which still use hot water and detergent, are powered by electricity and controlled by a microchip. This miniature electronic brain was developed in the late 1960s by American electrical engineer Marcian Edward (Ted) Hoff (1937–), working for the Intel Corporation.

Microchips have since found their way into all manner of household appliances. One of the most familiar is the microwave

Cold War Kitchen

After World War II ended in 1945, the world's two superpowers, the United States and the Soviet Union (now Russia and its neighboring republics), became locked in a hostile decades-long period of history known as the Cold War. Although fighting never broke out during that period, relations between the powers remained tense. Sometimes the rivalry spurred invention. When the Soviet Union launched its *Sputnik* space satellite in 1957, the United States was determined not to be outdone. Four years later, President John F. Kennedy announced his bold intention to put a man on the moon.

Former Soviet premier Nikita Khrushchev (*center left*) talks to then vice president Richard Nixon (*center right*) during their famous "kitchen debate" in 1959.

oven, developed in the early 1950s by American electrical engineer Percy Spencer (1894–1970). He was experimenting with radar, a type of radio used in ship and airplane navigation, when he found that radar's waves generated enough heat to melt a candy bar in his pocket. Spencer almost immediately began to concentrate on his accidental discovery—turning it into a revolutionary new technology for cooking food in a fraction of the time needed by conventional ovens.

At other times, the Cold War led to almost comical exchanges. Such was the case when Vice President Richard M. Nixon visited Moscow, Russia—the Soviet capital—in July 1959. During his stay, Nixon attended a US trade fair with the Soviet premier, Nikita Khrushchev. As they moved past a model home where the latest household appliances were on display, they began a lively debate about which of the world's two major political systems was better. Was it capitalism, as practiced by the United States, or communism, favored by the Soviet Union?

The "kitchen debate," as this came to be known, centered on household appliances. First, Nixon mentioned the invention of color television and insisted that his country had taken the lead with this technology. Khrushchev quickly replied that the Soviets had already developed the same idea. Next, Nixon stopped Khrushchev in a model of a kitchen with all the latest appliances. When Nixon proudly pointed out the latest American washing machine, Khrushchev quickly countered: "We have such things." Then Nixon pointed out a television that could be used to watch what was happening in different parts of the home, but Khrushchev was unimpressed: "Don't you have a machine that puts food into the mouth and pushes it down? Many things you've shown us are interesting but they are not needed in life. They have no useful purpose. They are merely gadgets." As they walked on, the two leaders continued a strange and lively war of words, intermingling mundane thoughts about domestic technology with the stern rhetoric of war and peace.

Bathroom Business

The bathroom contains a surprising number of inventions. One of the simplest, the nylon toothbrush, is actually a product of highly sophisticated modern chemistry. Nylon was developed in the 1930s by American chemist Wallace Carothers (1896–1937) and his coworkers. The technology behind nylon, called polymerization, involves building large molecules from many smaller ones based on the chemical element carbon. Apart from nylon toothbrushes, polymerization is used to make other modern plastics, including PVC (polyvinylchloride)—from which such objects as bathtub toys are manufactured.

Plastics are also used to make disposable safety razors, which were first developed in the late nineteenth century by King C. Gillette (1855–1932). Before the invention of the safety razor, most men shaved with "cutthroat" razors, which were like very sharp knives with rounded blades. These traditional razors were dangerous and needed regular sharpening. Gillette had the idea to make a razor with disposable blades that could be thrown out when they became dull.

The flush toilet is a central feature of every modern bathroom, and its present form was developed in 1775 by British inventor Alexander Cummings. Toilet paper—an even older invention—is believed to date from fourteenth-century China. Modern toilet paper has been manufactured in the United States since 1857, when Joseph Gayetty set up a factory specifically for making the product. Around 1880, the British Perforated Paper Company began making toilet paper in convenient, ready-cut squares. A century later, Japanese inventors developed "paperless" toilets. Ultra-hygienic, they are made from metals that resist bacteria and have an air dryer built in that entirely takes over the function of toilet paper.

End of Domesticity

Toward the end of the nineteenth century, the arrival of electric power began a new age that helped to liberate women from domestic chores. One invention played an especially important part: the electric motor. An electric motor uses electricity to generate magnetism, which makes the central part of the motor rotate so it can drive a machine. The basic principle of the motor was developed in 1821 by English scientist Michael Faraday (1791–1867) and turned into a more practical invention about ten years later by another Englishman, William Sturgeon (1783–1850). Motors soon made possible electrical appliances such as the vacuum cleaner (1901), food mixer (1904), washing machine (1909), electric dishwasher (1912), and modern refrigerator (1928).

Well into the twentieth century, women were the most likely members of their households to do the domestic chores, and, accordingly, they were the chief beneficiaries of household inventions. The corporations making domestic appliances knew this and advertised their products as both saving time and lightening labor. In 1917, for example, the General Electric Company sold its Mazda light as "The Lamp That Lights the Way to Lighter Housework." As a result of laborsaving devices, women had more time to devote to their family, for leisure, or to secure careers outside the home.

Today, people still spend a lot of time on household chores; however, new mechanisms make housework easier to complete, also giving people time to relax. There is no doubt that inventors of household items have revolutionized the way people manage their residences, clean, and unwind in their homes. Without these inventions, lifestyles across the globe would be very different.

Pioneer of the Video Game Industry

Nolan Bushnell

1943–

Inventions come in many shapes and sizes. Some have a small impact on society, while others completely change an industry. One inventor to influence the rise of a new generation of inventions was Nolan Bushnell. He created a video game, *Pong*, in 1972. With it, his company, Atari, dominated the computer industry for nearly two decades and introduced many people to the field of video gaming, which still exists today.

Beginnings

Nolan Bushnell was born February 5, 1943, in Ogden, Utah. As a boy, he repaired radios, television sets, and washing machines. After his father, a cement contractor, died when Bushnell was

Nolan Bushnell at WIRED BizCon in 2014

fifteen years old, Nolan took charge and completed his father's outstanding contracts. This early experience in the business world helped prepare him for a career as an **entrepreneur.**

After high school, Bushnell attended the University of Utah, graduating in 1968 with a degree in electrical engineering. During the summers, he worked in an amusement park, where he rose to the position of games arcade manager. In college, one of his professors introduced him to the relatively young field of computer graphics. He also became adept at chess, playing in several tournaments, and at the Japanese strategy game Go.

Defining the Problem

While in college, Bushnell had been one of several computer students who played the game *Spacewar!* This early video game, which was very simplistic in terms of strategy and graphics, sparked Bushnell's interest in creating a more interesting game for a wider audience. In the late 1960s, the only people outside the military who had access to computers and computer games were a few university students and professors. Although the average person knew little or nothing about computers at the time, Bushnell envisioned a video game that everyone could play.

In 1970, he formed a company, Syzygy, but when he found that that company name had already been taken, he had to register under a different name. He chose the name "Atari," a term in the game of Go that is similar to the term "check" in chess. Bushnell and his collaborator Ted Dabney developed the first arcade-style game, *Computer Space*, in 1971. Much as in *Spacewar!*, the player controlled a spaceship that was being attacked by aliens. Unfortunately, most players found the game too confusing, and *Computer Space* never became a big hit, although it did appear in a number of films, including *Jaws* (1975).

Designing the Solution

Bushnell realized that for a game to become popular it would need to be easy to learn, yet also provide continuing challenges to players as they became more proficient. His next invention satisfied this

Dawn of the Video Arcade

Nolan Bushnell did not invent the video game; he invented the idea of a culture in which people would get together to play video games—the video arcade. His interest in computer video games in college and his degree in electrical engineering gave him the technical preparation he would need to be a pioneer in the field. However, his larger vision about the place video games would assume in the culture is the foundation for Bushnell's importance in the history of invention.

By the time Bushnell encountered video games in the late 1960s, video game technology had been around for more than a decade. William Higinbotham, who worked at the Brookhaven National Laboratory, a nuclear research facility in Upton, New York, had developed in 1958 an oscilloscope that allowed two people to play against each other in a rudimentary form of table tennis. This simple "tennis for two," as Higinbotham called it, was demonstrated to only a few people at an in-house exposition in October 1958.

requirement supremely. After its first appearance in November 1972, *Pong,* which was an arcade version of Ping-Pong, became the first truly popular video game. Bushnell had the first *Pong* machine installed at a tavern, Andy Capp's, in Sunnyvale, California. It was so popular there that people were lining up outside the door to get a chance to play it.

Atari's *Pong* resembled *Odyssey,* a game that a company called Magnavox had released for the home video market in May 1972. Magnavox sued Atari, claiming that the idea for electronic Ping-Pong belonged to it. Atari decided to settle, agreeing to pay part of its profits to Magnavox.

Bushnell turned his attention to the home market. In 1974, Atari began to develop a version of *Pong* that could be connected to television sets and played on the television screen. It consisted of a box containing the game's electronics and handheld controls that moved an electronic paddle up and down on the screen to deflect an oncoming ball back to the opponent's court. The product was released in time for Christmas 1975, when it became the most popular gift of

Eight years later, Ralph Baer, an engineer, would take video game technology to another level when he introduced a system that could hook up to a home television set. The Magnavox Odyssey system, the first commercially available home video game system, released in 1972, was Baer's creation.

To many, including Nolan Bushnell, the graphics of the Magnavox Odyssey appeared rudimentary. The system even came with different-sized color overlays for television screens to depict the different playing fields, such as hockey and tennis. After Bushnell first saw the Odyssey at a trade show in California in the spring of 1972, he immediately realized the potential for such a game (with improved graphics) in restaurants, bars, and other public venues, which at that time offered only pinball machines. Later that year, his first *Pong* machine was installed in a tavern in California, where it became an enormous hit. Soon, *Pong* machines were appearing in similar locations across the United States.

the season. Bushnell had made a distribution agreement with Sears, greatly expanding its distribution and therefore its sales potential.

Applying the Solution

Although *Pong* was enormously successful, its popularity was relatively short-lived. People soon tired of it because they could play only the one game; they wanted a machine that could play several different games. As a result, in 1976 Bushnell and Atari prepared to release the Atari 2600. (They actually waited until 1977 to release this system because the settlement with Magnavox stipulated that Magnavox would receive part of Atari's profits through 1976.) This system had a slot into which players could insert different cartridges in order to play a wide range of games. The 2600 remained in production until 1992—a remarkable life span for a product in the rapidly changing video game industry. Other Atari systems produced during this period had similar life spans. Atari would go on to release versions of popular games such as *Asteroids*, *Millipede*, and *Lunar Lander*.

Bushnell sold Atari to Warner Communications in 1976, though he remained Atari's president. Not long after, however, he was forced out of the company, reportedly because he was at odds with Warner's stricter corporate environment (including a dress code to which Bushnell was opposed). Moreover, Bushnell opposed Warner's decision to have Atari enter the home computer market, preferring to see the company's computer research go into improving its video games. He left the company in 1978.

About a Mouse

When he left Atari and Warner, Bushnell took with him an idea that would become the next focus of his career. Bushnell was still at Atari when in 1977 he developed Pizza Time Theatre, a concept that would combine a video game arcade with a fast-food restaurant. He purchased an $800 animal costume and gave it to some of his engineers with the instruction to make a robotic animal character that could sing and talk. The result was Chuck E. Cheese. Since Atari was by then part of Warner, the decision on whether or not to pursue this idea was out of Bushnell's hands. When Warner showed little enthusiasm for Pizza Time Theatre (allowing only one to open), Bushnell purchased the rights from Warner and took the project forward on his own.

Bushnell envisioned a company that would combine elements of McDonald's and Disneyland, and that would rival them both in popularity. Customers could play video games or watch movies while eating fast food, or they could watch a live show put on by robotic animal characters.

The first Chuck E. Cheese's restaurant opened in San Jose, California, in 1977. That year, the Pizza Time Theatre Company reported earnings of just under $350,000. Within five years, annual revenues were more than $90 million. In the mid-1980s, however, with an industry-wide downturn in the video game industry, Chuck E. Cheese's fortunes sank as well. In 1984, Pizza Time Theatres filed for

Nolan Bushnell began Chuck E. Cheese's in 1977. Today, the company is still popular with kids around the United States.

bankruptcy, and Bushnell left the company. Eventually, the company revived, and Chuck E. Cheese's restaurants continue to operate in the United States and other countries into the twenty-first century.

The Impact of the Solution on Society

Bushnell went on to found several companies throughout the 1980s and 1990s. Among the more successful of these was Catalyst Technologies, which operated as a holding company for a number of other technology-oriented ventures. He had founded this enterprise in 1981 while still with Pizza Time Theatre. In effect, with Catalyst Technologies, Bushnell created a company to fund other inventors who required such material means as equipment and office space. Two of the companies that grew up under Catalyst's support were Axlon Inc., which created robotic toys, and Etak Inc., which produced computerized maps for automobiles. However, many of the companies that started under Catalyst Technologies became high-profile failures, such as Androbot, which sought to create robots for home use. Through it all, Bushnell always emerged confident in the potential for technology and video games to have positive social effects.

Like many observers of the video game industry and its growing place in society, Bushnell had begun to lament the tendency of video games to promote isolation and antisocial behavior. His original intent in creating *Pong*, he maintained, was to offer groups of people the opportunity to socialize in a context of fun and casual competition. Increasingly, however, video games were having just the opposite effect. In 2006, Bushnell reiterated his belief in the social good of technology when he announced his plan to open a series of restaurants where adults could get together and play video games over dinner. The new chain was to be called the uWink Media Bistro restaurant chain.

He had founded uWink.com in 1999 intending to develop an online video game, shopping, and entertainment network with terminals in various public venues. However, the Internet at that time was not advanced or stable enough to support uWink's vision, so this concept was sold and incorporated at a number of restaurants throughout the world. However, in 2010, the company announced it would shut down operations at all of its locations. It sold off its computer services to other stores, and by 2012, all uWink services had ended.

Nolan Bushnell wanted to "make computers do fun things," and his invention of *Pong* and the establishment of Atari did just that. It brought people together and changed the way games were played around the world. Bushnell's insight and entrepreneurial sense brought the computer and video gaming worlds together and inspired the expansion of the industry. It is because of him and his endeavors that the video gaming and computer industries continue today.

Timeline

1943
Nolan Bushnell born in Ogden, Utah

1968
Bushnell graduates from the University of Utah with a degree in electrical engineering

1970
Bushnell forms the company Atari

1971
Bushnell and Ted Dabney develop *Computer Space*

1972
Bushnell invents *Pong*

1977
Atari releases the Atari 2600; Bushnell opens first Chuck E. Cheese's

1978
Bushnell leaves Atari

1984
Bushnell leaves Pizza Time Theatre

1999
Bushnell develops uWink.com

Inventor of Air-Conditioning

Willis Carrier

1876–1950

On a hot summer's day nothing feels better than going from the furnace of outdoors into a cool environment with air-conditioning. The device was developed in 1902 by Willis Carrier, a mechanical engineer, and it would have a profound effect on the way people lived and worked. Since its beginnings, air-conditioning has transformed societies. In the United States, many people cannot fathom living through a summer without it. Its ability to make environments much cooler than the air outside makes many people dependent on it, especially during hot days. Today, Willis Carrier is a name that lives on, as namesake of the company he started and the father of one of the most important inventions of recent times.

An Inventor's Start

Willis Haviland Carrier was born November 26, 1876, in Angola, New York, near Lake Erie. An only child from a modest farm family, Carrier showed an early interest in mechanical objects, apparently inheriting his aptitude for tinkering from his Quaker mother, who died when he was eleven years old. Carrier worked his way through high school, then taught for three years while trying to earn enough money to go to college. In 1895, he won a scholarship to attend Cornell University in Ithaca, New York. He graduated in 1901 with a degree in mechanical engineering.

Willis Carrier in 1915

Defining the Problem

Carrier's first job was with the Buffalo Forge Company, which designed and manufactured heating, blower, and air exhaust systems. He went to work in the heating engineering department, designing systems for heating and drying a variety of things, including coffee and lumber. After devising improved methods for measuring the capacity of heating systems, Carrier became director of the department in charge of experimental engineering. He found that the existing data for measuring heating capacity were poorly calculated and prevented designing efficient heating and air ventilation systems. Therefore, before he attempted to create any improved systems, he started from the beginning and reexamined everything he knew about the nature of airflow and humidity.

Designing the Solution

Armed with a better understanding of the relationship between air temperature and humidity, Carrier faced his first major challenge.

Around the time Carrier joined Buffalo Forge, the Sackett-Wilhelms Lithographing and Publishing Company of Brooklyn, New York, contracted Buffalo Forge to improve air conditions in its plant. Changes in the heat and humidity levels inside the plant had been causing the printer's paper supplies to expand and contract, making it impossible to align colored inks properly. Carrier devised a control system to regulate heat and humidity in the plant.

By releasing steam from the plant's main boilers at low pressure into perforated pipes, he was able to introduce humidity into the air during the dry winter months. For the humid days of summer, Carrier's design featured a system whereby air was blown over two sets of coils: one through which cool well water flowed, another that was refrigerated by an ammonia compressor. Through these means, Carrier managed to stabilize the atmosphere inside the factory to a level of 55 percent relative humidity throughout the year, maintaining a temperature of 70 degrees Fahrenheit (21 degrees Celsius) in winter and 80°F (26°C) in summer. Carrier received a patent for his "Apparatus for Treating Air" in 1906.

Applying the Solution

After his success at Sackett-Wilhelms, Carrier went on to design similar systems for other industrial environments, making several improvements along the way. By 1907, his systems had been installed in cotton and paper mills and in food processing and pharmaceutical manufacturing plants, among other places. That same year, the Buffalo Forge Company established a wholly owned subsidiary, the Carrier Air Conditioning Company. Its purpose was to design, market, and install complete air-conditioning systems. Carrier was appointed vice president of this company as well as its chief engineer and director of research.

Buffalo Forge withdrew from the engineering business in 1914 to focus its energies on manufacturing. In 1915, Carrier and a few of his colleagues formed the Carrier Engineering Corporation. By this time, he was being called the father of air-conditioning because of the great success he had had installing systems in a wide range of buildings. The term "air-conditioning" was coined by a mill owner in Charlotte,

North Carolina, named Stuart Cramer. Carrier soon adopted the term for his own marketing campaigns to describe the overall control of air humidity, temperature, and flow.

New Inventions

To this point, however, Carrier's air-conditioning systems had been designed and implemented to meet industrial needs; their chief aim was to regulate the way air might affect manufacturing processes and goods. Carrier felt that his invention would eventually be adopted specifically for human comfort, but so far his only clients were in the industrial sector, in great part because of the high cost of his systems. This was about to change, however. Soon after Carrier started his own corporation, he invented a device that could use refrigerants to cool and blow air in a manner far less costly than his big industrial installations. This device, the centrifugal compressor, also referred to as the centrifugal chiller, became the basis for the modern air conditioner as well as refrigeration systems of all kinds. The transformation of Carrier's designs for application to a broad range of human uses had begun.

The Impact of the Solution on Society

Carrier air-conditioning systems were soon showing up in buildings all over America. An important early example was in the J. L. Hudson department store in Detroit, Michigan, in 1924. Carrier developed the first home air conditioner in 1928. In 1928 and 1929, he installed air-conditioning in the House and Senate chambers of the Capitol in Washington, DC. By that time, the Carrier Engineering Corporation operated two plants: one in Newark, New Jersey, and another in Allentown, Pennsylvania. By the end of the 1920s, Carrier's systems were beginning to have a greater effect on a wider segment of the American population: more than three hundred movie theaters across the country had air-conditioning installed by 1930.

In 1930, Carrier Engineering Corporation merged with the Brunswick-Kroeschell Company and the York Heating and Ventilating Corporation. The new company, called the Carrier Corporation, appointed Willis Carrier as the chairman of its board of directors. Carrier's success was slowed during the Great Depression, and he was forced to take severe measures to ensure his company's survival. He brought in financial and personnel consultants, cut staffing and costs, implemented more efficient workflows, and consolidated all the company's operations in Syracuse, New York.

Throughout these financial woes, Carrier always insisted on funding further research and development, knowing that advances in air-conditioning technology to suit a wider range of applications were essential to his company's success. Specifically, he focused on high-rise buildings. Unlike large factories or warehouses spread out horizontally over a vast area of land, the new vertical high-rise buildings could not sacrifice any space to the large ducts and bulky

Humidity

Willis Carrier's main contribution as an inventor was to create a machine that could pump cool air into homes and workplaces. His original mission, however, had less to do with achieving lower air temperatures than it did with lowering the humidity level of the air. His first major breakthrough came in 1902, when he solved the problems faced by the Sackett-Wilhelms Lithographing and Publishing Company, which found its paper stock expanding or contracting depending on the moisture level inside its printing plant. From this experience, Carrier sought to better understand the relationship between air temperature and humidity.

One foggy day in 1904, while he was waiting on a railroad platform for his train to arrive, he began to reflect upon the quality of the air around him. Realizing that fog is actually water vapor condensed from air, he reasoned that air temperature determines how much water vapor air can contain. The ability of air to hold water vapor becomes higher at higher temperatures and lower at lower temperatures. Carrier concluded that if he were to find a way to cool humid air, he could reduce its water vapor content. His solution was coils that ran the length of ceilings in shorter buildings. In 1939, Carrier developed a system that featured a central station within a high-rise from which conditioned air was piped through small steel **conduits** at rapid speed. These conduits carried the air over additional heating or cooling coils, depending on the season, before delivering it through nozzles into individual rooms.

The technology was widely praised, although installations were generally slowed by World War II, when American manufacturing and resources were devoted to the war effort rather than to comfortable office air. After the war ended in 1945, an unparalleled boom in the housing and office building market occurred as both returning soldiers and workers at home resumed more normal lives and started new jobs. This boom carried over into the market for air conditioners. Air-conditioning was now considered compulsory for office buildings as well as many homes. The Carrier Corporation was at the head of this explosion.

somewhat paradoxical: by spraying cold water through the humid air, he could reduce the air's water vapor level and at the same time reduce its temperature. This happened because when the additional water was sprayed through the humid air, it raised the water vapor level to a point that exceeded the maximum amount of water vapor that air can contain. The water vapor then condensed, turning to water. Outside, this natural process results in dew forming on leaves and grass. In an air conditioner, the result is the drip of water that comes out the back of a window unit and sometimes falls on the heads of pedestrians below.

Although the reduction of air humidity was at first the only concern among purchasers of Carrier's products, Carrier insisted that the resultant effect of lowering temperature would be an even greater draw. He was right. On a scorching hot day, nearly everyone in America plans activities around access to air-conditioning. Movie theaters, malls, department stores—these are just a few of the places that have capitalized on air-conditioning.

THE PERFECT ENVIRONMENT

No open windows—ample fresh air

With the Carrier Self-Contained Unit Air Conditioner in your office or home
you can keep your windows permanently closed—shutting out noise, dust and
dirt—and enjoy real fresh air throughout the year—pre-selected warm temperature in winter with the desired moisture automatically added, and cool in summer
with the excess moisture removed. The fresh, conditioned air is filtered and
circulated without draughts, and the vitiated air removed.

Carrier

Unit air conditioners

require no structural alterations

A postcard will bring you a complete range of interesting literature

CARRIER WEATHERMAKERS LTD., 27 Conduit Street W.1

Telephone: Mayfair 4420 and 0351

This advertisement for Carrier air conditioners
appeared in 1937.

The Legend Lives On

By the time he died of a heart attack on October 7, 1950, Willis
Carrier held more than eighty patents. Carrier's inventions are
credited with contributing to some of the broadest changes in
American and global culture. One of these has been the migration
of a significant number of Americans to southern and southwestern
states that prior to air-conditioning were considered by many to be
unlivable during the summer. In this sense, the opening of the Sunbelt
can be attributed to Carrier's air-conditioning.

Air-conditioning has changed the way people operate inside and
outside the home. Prior to its creation and popularity, people spent
more time outdoors during the long summer months. Since the early
1900s, however, as air-conditioning units improved and became more

accessible—especially inside houses and apartments—more people spent time inside, cooling off.

Carrier's invention influenced the way people managed their time and greatly improved living conditions for people around the world. In extremely warm climates, air-conditioning is especially important to the people living there. Carrier's legacy continues to this day, and the Carrier Corporation he founded remains a leader in the world's air-conditioning, heating, and ventilation systems.

Timeline

1876
Willis Haviland Carrier born in Angola, New York

1901
Carrier graduates from Cornell University and joins the Buffalo Forge Company

1907
The Carrier Air Conditioning Company is established

1915
Carrier forms the Carrier Engineering Corporation with some colleagues

1928
Carrier develops the first home air conditioner

1930
Carrier appointed chairman of the new Carrier Corporation

1939
Carrier develops an air-conditioning system for high-rise buildings

1950
Carrier dies

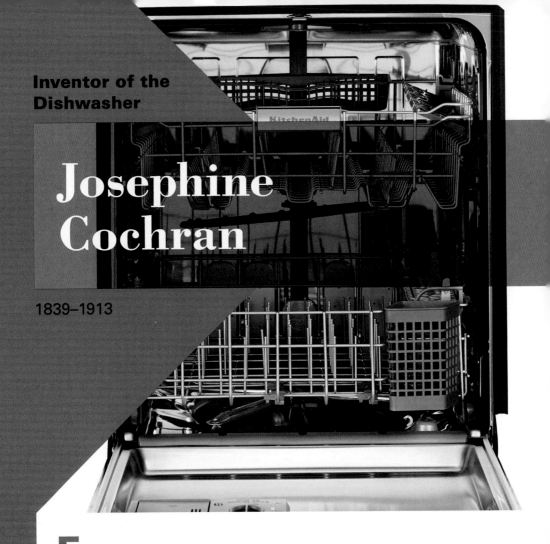

Josephine Cochran

1839–1913

For centuries men and women have contributed remarkable ideas for innovative products. Often, due to the nature of the times in which they lived, women had more difficulty getting their inventions recognized. However, women did not let social circumstances keep them from having their voices and ideas heard. With persistence and determination, they succeeded. One unlikely inventor was Josephine Cochran. She had no formal education in engineering or mechanics, and yet she designed one of the most innovative concepts of the nineteenth century—the dishwasher. Her invention changed the way people cleaned and spurred a kind of industrial revolution within the household.

Josephine Cochran

Daughter of an Engineer

Cochran was born Josephine Garis in Ashtabula County, Ohio, in 1839. She was the daughter of John Garis, a respected civil engineer who was active in the development of Chicago during the 1850s. She was also the great-granddaughter of John Fitch, an inventor of a steamboat who committed suicide when he lost the necessary financing to market his invention. Josephine never knew her great-grandfather, but he was highly regarded by her family, who considered him a great, if tragic, genius.

While Josephine was growing up, her father supervised mills along the Ohio River. Later the family moved to Valparaiso, Indiana, where her father worked for the state as an engineer. After her mother died, Josephine's father sent her to Illinois to live with one of her sisters. There, she met William Cochran, whom she married in 1858, when she was nineteen and he was twenty-seven.

William Cochran was from Shelbyville, Illinois, and he was already a well-off dry-goods merchant when Josephine married him. Soon after their marriage, they moved back to Shelbyville, where William Cochran's affable manner and respectable family eased his entry into politics. He soon became a force in Shelbyville's Democratic Party and was elected county circuit clerk four times.

Defining the Problem

Social connections were important to William Cochran's political career, so Josephine Cochran frequently entertained at their home. In the early 1880s, Cochran noticed that her best china—a treasured family heirloom—had been chipped by servants doing the dishwashing. Cochran was so upset about the damage that from that time forward she refused to allow the servants to wash the dishes, doing the job herself.

She soon discovered that she truly hated washing dishes. She later recalled finding the job tedious and unpleasant, and she thought that the hot water and soap were ruining her hands. Cochran finally returned the job to the servants, whose prior carelessness left her feeling ill at ease.

Someone, she thought, should build a machine that washed dishes, saving people from the trouble and saving dishes from damage. As no such machine existed, Cochran decided to invent one herself. Once Cochran made the decision, she later recalled, she sat in her library examining a cup and within about half an hour, she had thought up the basic plan for her dishwashing machine. Her idea was to create a machine that would mimic the steps of washing by hand—first applying soapy water to the dishes, then rinsing them, and then drying them with hot air—while all the time holding the dishes in wire racks so that they would not be damaged.

She told her friends about her idea, and they strongly encouraged her to develop it. Their enthusiasm demonstrated to Cochran that there would be demand for such a machine if it could be invented. In addition, her husband was well connected and influential, and Cochran believed it would be easy for her to get financial backing to produce and market a mechanical dishwasher once she built a working **prototype**. Cochran was so excited about the idea that, in 1883, when her husband left Shelbyville seeking to improve his ailing health, she stayed home to work on the design of her machine.

William Cochran came back early, however, having fallen severely ill. He died two weeks later. When his will was read, Cochran discovered that her husband had left her the paltry sum of $1,500 ($36,932 US dollars in 2014)—and outstanding debts of $2,800 (around $68,940 US dollars in 2014). Cochran was now a widow and virtually penniless.

Designing the Solution

Cochran was left with a house that had a shed behind it and an idea for a dishwashing machine. She began to build the machine in the shed, enlisting the expertise of George Butters, a railroad mechanic who helped Cochran construct the prototype. Within months, Cochran had a working dishwashing machine. In December 1886, she received US Patent No. 355,139 for the machine, which she would call the Garis-Cochran Dish Washing Machine. Now she had to manufacture and market her new invention. "If I knew all I know today when I began to put the dishwasher on the market," she later remarked, "I never would have had the courage to start."

Applying the Solution

At first, Cochran tried selling the device to housewives. However, the machines were expensive. As Cochran later noted, in the typical late-nineteenth-century household, the husband was the one who decided what new machines were worth spending money on—and he was not the one doing the dishes.

In 1887, Cochran decided to travel to Chicago to try to sell a bigger version of her machine to large hotels and institutions. Although her husband's death meant that she had less influence, she still had social connections. Before she left, she wrote letters to everyone she knew in Chicago. One of Cochran's Chicago friends responded, offering to introduce her to the manager of the Palmer House, then one of the biggest and most famous hotels in that city. Cochran met the manager and sold him her novel machine.

Then she decided to try the Sherman House, another huge, well-known Chicago hotel. She did not know anybody at that hotel, however, and she had to make her first "cold" business call, walking into the hotel alone and asking to see the manager. It was an intimidating task for a woman raised with nineteenth-century notions of ladylike behavior. "That was almost the hardest thing I ever did, I think, crossing the great lobby of the Sherman House alone," she later recalled. "You cannot imagine what it was like in those days ... for a woman to cross a hotel lobby alone. I had never been anywhere without my husband or father—the lobby seemed a mile wide. I thought I should faint at every step, but I didn't—and I got an $800 order as my reward."

The Palmer and Sherman accounts not only brought Cochran much-needed money, they proved vital to the marketing of the Garis-Cochran Dish Washing Machine. Both hotels had strong national reputations, and the fact that they used Cochran's machines helped persuade other hotels to adopt the new technology.

Indeed, hotels were among the earliest and most enthusiastic purchasers of the Cochran dishwashers, which could wash and dry 240 dishes in less than two minutes. Each machine cost the equivalent of several thousand dollars in today's money, but most hotels made the money back in a matter of months because they needed a smaller dishwashing staff and fewer dishes were broken.

Although Cochran was able to market her machines on her own, she could not manufacture them alone, and she did not have the money to construct a factory. Instead, she entered into an agreement with E.B. Tait, a firm in Decatur, Indiana, to build the machines on a contract basis. That arrangement ultimately proved a source of great frustration to Cochran; she had many ideas to improve her machines,

Working Cochran's Invention

Patents for dishwashing machines had been issued some thirty years before the Garis-Cochran Dish Washing Machine was invented in 1886. Cochran's dishwashing machine differed from the others in two important ways: it was easier to manufacture, and it actually left dishes clean and unbroken.

Other inventors had tried to create mechanical dish scrubbers, which were too complicated to manufacture on a large scale, or they tried to move the dishes around from wash basin to rinse basin, a process that led to breakage. In a Garis-Cochran Dish Washing Machine, the dishes stayed still—firmly held in wire baskets that were shaped to fit plates, bowls, cups, and glasses. Instead of relying on mechanical scrubbers, Cochran relied on scalding hot, soapy water.

Her machines sprayed hot, soapy water onto the dishes to wash them, then rinsed them with sprays of hot, clear water. The machine then blew hot air on the dishes to dry them. The purpose of this design was simply to ensure clean, unbroken dishes, but an unexpected benefit was that a Cochran dishwashing machine sanitized the dishes as well as cleaned them—providing hospitals and other large institutions with yet another reason to purchase her invention.

but the Tait management tended to dismiss them because she was a woman with no formal technical education.

Nonetheless, her business continued to grow. In 1893, the World's Columbian Exposition, better known as the world's fair, was held in Chicago. The massive fair, held to celebrate the four-hundredth anniversary of Christopher Columbus's voyage to the Americas, was incredibly popular, attracting more than twenty-seven million visitors during the six months it was open. That many people produced a lot of dirty dishes, and nine Garis-Cochran Dish Washing Machines were used by restaurants at the fair. In addition, Cochran's dishwashing machine was awarded the top prize in a competition held at the fair to judge inventions. The prize, the performance of the machines at the fair, and the fact that they had been invented by a woman created significant publicity for Cochran.

Sales increased enough that, in 1898, Cochran was finally able to build a factory of her own near Chicago, hiring Butters—who had helped her build the prototype—as foreman. Sales continued to grow in the early twentieth century, as more and more hotels, department stores, hospitals, restaurants, and colleges bought dishwashing machines. Cochran continued to run her business, traveling to meet clients and woo new ones, until her death in 1913 at age seventy-four.

The Impact of the Solution on Society

After Cochran's death, her company underwent changes in name and ownership, finally becoming KitchenAid. Dishwashing machines have changed, too, but Cochran's basic concept, in which water is sprayed onto dishes held in wire racks, is still used today.

One change in the market for dishwashers that doubtless would have pleased Cochran was the adoption of dishwashing machines in the home. Cochran tried throughout her lifetime to get her dishwashers used in private homes, building smaller machines and advertising them vigorously, but until the 1950s, dishwashing machines were used almost exclusively by institutions.

One reason was cost, but other factors also came into play. During Cochran's lifetime, most people did not have the large, powerful water heaters needed to supply such a machine with adequate amounts of

This woman models a dishwasher in Paris in 1930.

scalding water. In addition, the dishwashing soap used before the advent of detergents in the 1940s tended to leave a scum on the dishes. Once water heater and soap technology caught up, the dishwashing machine became a common home appliance; in modern times, some 56 percent of American homes have dishwashing machines.

As dishwashing machines—along with other labor-saving domestic appliances, such as the clothes-washing machine, the electric iron, and the vacuum cleaner—became more common from the 1950s onward, Cochran's invention eventually did what she had always hoped it would do. It allowed people, women in particular, to spend less time on household chores and freed them to use their energy and time to engage in other activities that they found more satisfying.

Today, many households have dishwashing machines. They have been a beneficial part of modern homes and have made cleaning up after meals less stressful. Without Josephine Cochran and her solution to a tedious chore, many homes around the world would be quite different. Cochran's vision and subsequent determination to make it a reality testified to society that not only was a woman capable of inventing a highly useful product, but that she could also bring it to life and make it a lasting device.

Timeline

1839
Josephine Garis born in Ohio

1858
Garis marries William Cochran

1886
Josephine Cochran patents her dishwasher

1887
Cochran sells her first machine to a Chicago hotel called the Palmer House

1893
Cochran's dishwasher wins a major inventing award at the world's fair in Chicago

1898
Cochran builds her own factory

1913
Cochran dies

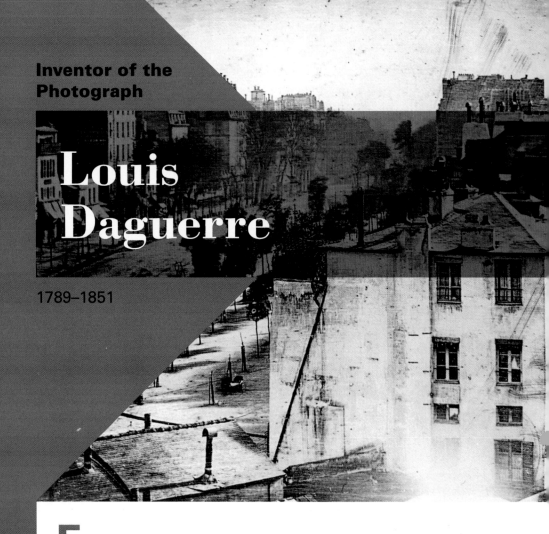

Inventor of the Photograph

Louis Daguerre

1789–1851

Ever since humans first walked the earth they have been trying to capture the world around them as they see it. Up until the nineteenth century, this was only possible through drawing or painting. The invention of the camera in the 1830s signaled a new era in human history, an era in which humans could capture themselves in a way no one had previously thought possible: as they appear in everyday life. This invention, first developed by Louis Daguerre, changed the world forever and challenged others to improve on the product, eventually making it into what we know today.

Makings of an Inventor

Louis-Jacques-Mandé Daguerre was born in Cormeilles-en-Parisis near Paris, France, in 1789. Little is known about his early life and education. Although he started working as a tax collector, he was soon earning his living in more creative ways. He worked as an architect's apprentice for a time and then, at age sixteen, became a scene painter and set designer. From 1819 to 1822, he was set designer at the Paris Opera, where he painted huge landscape backdrops and designed unique lighting effects. *Aladdin or the Marvelous Lamp* was a notable production in 1822, in which Daguerre was the first to use gas lamps to light the stage.

Louis Daguerre in 1844

Daguerre's theater work inspired his first business idea, the Diorama, in 1822. Working with his friend Charles-Marie Bouton, he painted enormous pictures of dramatic or famous events on translucent paper, typically 45 × 71 feet (13.7 meters × 21.6 meters). Then he positioned lights around and behind the pictures, switching the lights on and off to suggest changes in the weather or time of day. Adding music, animals, actors, props, and special effects, he created breathtaking scenes that people paid to view. The scenes Daguerre painted had titles like *Land-Slip in the Valley of Goldau* and *Cathedral of Sainte Marie de Montréal* and were based on real-life places and happenings. In order to be effective, the diorama scenes had to be painted as realistically as possible. This led Daguerre to wonder if there were better ways of copying the things he saw.

Defining the Problem

The very same question had already occurred to Joseph-Nicéphore Niépce (1765–1833). Beginning around 1814, Niépce had tried to find ways of capturing sunlight on paper. He began by using a simple device called a camera obscura that artists had been using since at least 1500. This device can be a large darkened room with a tiny hole in the drapes or a huge sealed box or chamber with a small hole in one wall. When light enters through the hole, it throws an image of the outside world onto the opposite wall inside. There was nothing in a camera obscura that could record light. Instead, artists would hang pieces of paper on the wall and then sketch around the image they saw to record it. However, during the eighteenth century, several chemists, including the German Johann Schulze (1687–1744) and the Swede Carl Scheele (1742–1786), discovered that some chemicals based on silver changed color when they were left out in the light. This discovery opened up the possibility of using chemicals in a camera obscura to record images.

In 1827, Niépce combined these two ideas and made the world's first photograph. First, he prepared what was called a **photographic plate**. Then he put the plate upright inside a camera obscura and left it by the window of his house. Very slowly, over about eight hours, the plate captured a fairly blurred image of the view from his window (a process known as exposing the plate to light). Niépce called his invention heliography, which means "drawing by the sun."

Daguerre had also started experimenting with chemicals to see if he could capture sunlight permanently on paper. He learned of Niépce's work and wrote to him on December 14, 1829. The two men became partners, hoping they would develop a quick and easy way of capturing sunlight on paper. When they switched to using copper plates and a light-sensitive chemical based on iodine, they managed to cut the exposure time from eight hours to twenty or thirty minutes, but otherwise their results were not much better.

Designing the Solution

After Niépce died in July 1833, Daguerre continued his experiments with the help of Niépce's son, Isidore. A couple of years later, he made a dramatic breakthrough and discovered a better way of capturing light on photographic plates. There is a story that Daguerre threw some partly exposed plates into a closet where there was a broken thermometer. When he looked at the plates a few days later, he found an image had formed on them. Daguerre realized that the mercury from the thermometer was the cause: the vapor it had given off had somehow "fixed" the image onto the metal plates. However, historians of photography think this story was probably made up later; no one really knows how Daguerre discovered the importance of mercury.

However it happened, Daguerre had arrived at a much better way of taking pictures. It involved several stages. First, he took a copper plate, covered it in silver, and treated it with iodine vapor. This caused a chemical reaction that coated the plate with silver iodide, a light-sensitive compound. Daguerre put the plate in his camera and exposed it to light. Next, he "developed" the plate (revealed the image it contained) by letting fumes from hot mercury pass over it. Finally, he "fixed" the developed image (made it permanent) by treating it with common salt. The whole process was much quicker than anything that had been previously used.

Isidore Niépce was delighted. On November 1, 1837, he wrote to Daguerre: "What a difference … between the method which you employ and the one by which I toil on! While I require almost a whole day to make one design, you ask only four minutes! What an enormous advantage! It is so great, indeed, that no person, knowing both methods, would employ the old one." Niépce realized that Daguerre had made a breakthrough and, as a result, allowed his partner to name their new way of recording pictures the daguerreotype process.

A Negative to a Positive

Photography turns everyone into an artist: few people can paint a good portrait of a friend or a landscape that they love, but anyone can take a photograph. Louis Daguerre was inspired to invent the daguerreotype when he realized he could not draw quite as well as he would have liked. Exactly the same reasoning inspired the Englishman who invented the modern photographic process. William Henry Fox Talbot (1800–1877) was sketching lakes in Italy when he decided there had to be a better way of recording nature.

Unlike Louis Daguerre, Talbot tried to record images on paper, not metal, but he used silver compounds to capture light in a very similar

A calotype, or Talbotype (pictured here), was another popular method by which to produce photographs.

Applying the Solution

If Louis Daguerre and Niépce thought they were going to make their fortune, they were soon disappointed. When Daguerre tried to sell their invention, no one wanted to buy it. Luckily, there was interest of a different kind. On January 9, 1839, Daguerre demonstrated his invention at a meeting of the French Academy of Sciences;

way. He made his photographic paper by soaking it in common salt and then silver nitrate. A chemical reaction happened on the paper, coating it with light-sensitive silver chloride. Talbot placed the now-sensitive paper in the back of a camera, opened the lens to light for a minute or so to take a picture, then covered the lens again. Unlike the daguerreotype process, Talbot's process burned a ghostly negative image onto the paper: dark areas in the original picture showed up light and vice versa. Talbot then took the negative into a darkened room and treated it with other chemicals to produce a positive print in which the original light and dark areas were now reversed and showed up correctly.

Talbot announced his invention in 1839, the same year the French government made public Daguerre's process. The two men immediately became rivals. The best thing about Talbot's photographs (called Talbotypes or calotypes) was that the negative could be used to make any number of positive prints—something that was not possible with daguerreotypes. Whereas daguerreotypes were pin-sharp, Talbot's method produced softer and more artistic prints that many people thought too blurred. Daguerreotypes were free for anyone to use, thanks to the French government, but Talbot patented his process and tried to charge people for using it.

Daguerre gained the early advantage, but Talbot's process—and the improved wet-plate process developed by Frederick Scott Archer—eventually triumphed and evolved into the photographic film process still used today. It is ironic that Louis Daguerre remains more famous than William Henry Fox Talbot. Daguerre's original, metal-plate photographs have lasted longer and are now considered to be important historical records.

the audience was astonished by the incredible detail in the pictures he showed. Around this time, Daguerre's invention caught the attention of François Arago, a respected scientist and politician. He saw the potential immediately and came up with a novel suggestion: the French government should buy the rights to the daguerreotype and "then nobly give to the whole world this discovery which could contribute so much to the progress of art and science."

On June 15, 1839, the government set up a commission to consider the idea. Chaired by painter and art expert Paul Delaroche, the commission unanimously endorsed the plan about six weeks later. One said the daguerreotype was a "beautiful discovery." Delaroche saw it as the beginning of a whole new era in the visual arts, boldly declaring: "From today, painting is dead."

According to the terms of the deal, the French Academy of Sciences gained the rights to the daguerreotype and made the invention free for anyone to use. Accordingly, Daguerre wrote a detailed description of the invention—*An Historical and Descriptive Account of the Various Processes of the Daguerreotype and the Diorama*—which was published that August. In return for giving his invention to the government, he was made an officer of the Legion of Honor (a prestigious French award). He was also given a modest annual payment of 6,000 francs (equivalent to about $21,000 US in 2014), and Isidore Niépce was given 4,000 francs (equivalent to $14,000 US in 2014) to recognize his father's important work.

"I have seized the light, I have arrested its flight."
—Louis Daguerre

Once Daguerre's invention was made available to all, other inventors looked at ways of improving the process. Daguerre himself did little more. Instead, he returned to his first love, painting, and enjoyed a long retirement on his government pension. When he died at Bru-sur-Marne, France, on July 10, 1851, an obituary in the *Illustrated London News*, an English weekly, noted: "He was a man of extreme modesty and great personal worth, and devoted to his profession, that of an artist."

The Impact of the Solution on Society

The impact of Daguerre's invention was immediate. His booklet was an instant, international best seller. By the end of 1839, it had been published in a dozen languages in twenty-nine different editions. In the United States, Daguerre's process was popularized by the artist Samuel Morse (1791–1872), who became even more famous as the inventor of the electric telegraph. The process was later improved by scientist John William Draper (1811–1882). It spread rapidly when many people began to set themselves up as photographers specializing in daguerreotype, offering to capture portraits on shiny metal plates for around two to five dollars each. Millions of these cameo portraits had been taken by the 1850s.

Although the daguerreotype remained popular for about twenty years, it was eventually overtaken by better methods of photography. In England, William Henry Fox Talbot developed the modern photographic negative process. This allowed many copies to be made from an original image, something that was not possible with the daguerreotype. Talbot's method took a long time to catch on, and it was later improved by another English scientist, Frederick Scott Archer (1813–1857). Instead of using metal plates covered with dry chemicals, Archer coated his wet plates with liquid chemicals; although messier, they produced sharper images much more quickly and led eventually to the modern photographic film, developed by George Eastman (1854–1932) in 1883.

Together, these pioneers of photography made history by changing the way history was recorded. Until the invention of photography, history was mostly about the written word and the painted picture. Photography was something entirely different: it actually captured moments of history, as people saw them and as they were happening. Thanks to Niépce, Daguerre, and their colleagues, humankind now has a photographic record of many important events, including photographs from when astronauts first set foot on the moon and when the Berlin Wall was torn down. In addition to recording significant events in human history, photographs also allow people to capture memories of their own lives and families. Today, photography is everywhere—in books, newspapers, magazines, and billboards—and is taken entirely for granted.

While Louis Daguerre was not the first person to invent photography—Niépce had already developed a significant part of the process—he did make a truly remarkable discovery that lasted for decades and influenced others, such as Talbot, to find other methods of achieving similar results. The daguerreotype influenced the way people recorded moments of their lives and led to many great, related inventions, eventually culminating in current technologies such as smartphone cameras.

Timeline

1789
Louis Daguerre born in Cormeilles-en-Parisis, France

1814
Joseph-Nicéphore Niépce begins his work on photography

1819
Daguerre becomes a set designer at the Paris Opera

1822
With Charles-Marie Boulton, Daguerre creates the Diorama

1827
Niépce creates the first photograph

1829
Daguerre contacts Niépce, and they become partners

1833
Niépce dies; Daguerre continues his experiments; Daguerre creates the first daguerreotype

1839
Daguerre demonstrates his daguerreotype process to the French Academy of Sciences to great acclaim

1851
Daguerre dies

George
de Mestral

1907–1990

Sometimes inventors start out with an idea in their heads of what their invention will be like and how it should be created. In the course of inventing, however, sometimes all does not go to plan, and original ideas turn into accidental inventions of entirely different, although useful, devices. Such is the case with George de Mestral and the invention of hook-and-loop fasteners. De Mestral was looking for a new kind of fastening device when he began experimenting, and he soon stumbled upon an invention that would become quite popular and remain so even today.

De Mestral's hometown of Lausanne, Switzerland

An Inventor's Beginnings

De Mestral was born in 1907, in a small town outside of Lausanne, Switzerland, not far from Geneva, the country's capital. He exhibited an inventor's spirit early—by age twelve, he had already designed and patented a toy airplane. He attended the Swiss Federal Institute of Technology (École Polytechnique Fédérale de Lausanne), one of the premier universities in Europe, and earned a degree in electrical engineering.

After graduation, de Mestral began work as an engineer, starting in the machine shop of a local firm. His love for the outdoors led to his becoming an amateur mountaineer.

Defining the Problem

During one excursion in the Swiss mountains in 1941, de Mestral took special note of the burrs that had become attached to his wool pants and tangled in his dog's fur. The burrs were relatively small in size, but clung tenaciously to clothing and fur—so tenaciously, in fact, that they sometimes had to be cut off.

Intrigued by the burrs' strength, de Mestral examined one under a microscope. What he saw was a maze of hundreds of tiny hooks that snared the woven threads in cloth or strands of animal hair. One tiny hook seemed insignificant and had little strength, but hundreds of hooks together were quite powerful.

Others may have written off the burrs as a nuisance, but de Mestral saw them as an opportunity. He believed he could invent a new type of practical fastener based on the hook-and-loop principle of the burr.

Designing the Solution

Despite the simplicity of the burr's design, de Mestral needed nearly ten years to create the world's first hook and loop fastener. Frustrated with his initial attempts to create a type of hook-and-loop "tape" using the burr principle, de Mestral sought out the expertise of a French fabric weaver and a Swiss loom maker.

The first prototypes were made of cotton, which did not offer the kind of strength de Mestral had marveled at with the burrs. De Mestral then discovered nylon.

Nylon, a revolutionary type of synthetic fiber invented by Wallace Carothers (1896–1937) in the 1930s and dubbed the miracle fiber, was well known for its strength and durability. While experimenting with this new fiber, de Mestral discovered that when nylon was sewn under infrared light, it hardened, and when the fibers were cut, they formed nearly indestructible hooks.

Even with the new nylon technology, perfecting his invention took time. At first, the loops were the wrong size for the hooks, or vice versa; finding the perfect angle at which to cut the nylon fabric was a time-consuming challenge. Finally, VELCRO® brand fasteners were born.

De Mestral applied for a patent from the Swiss government in 1951. His prototype consisted of two strips of nylon with roughly three hundred hooks per square inch on one side and three hundred loops on the other. De Mestral was granted US Patent No. 2,717,437 in 1955.

Applying the Solution

De Mestral founded Velcro S.A. in Switzerland in 1952 and soon after opened a factory in Aubonne, Switzerland. By the late 1950s, de Mestral had been granted patents not just in the United States but also in other countries throughout Europe and Canada. Factories were established throughout the Western Hemisphere. The US factory, which remains in operation to this day, began producing VELCRO® brand fasteners in Manchester, New Hampshire, in 1958.

The Impact of the Solution on Society

De Mestral believed VELCRO® brand fasteners would revolutionize the garment industry, replacing standard clothing fasteners such as zippers and buttons. However, his invention was poorly received at first. The garment industry shunned VELCRO® brand fasteners, claiming they were too unsightly to use on clothing. For many years, de Mestral earned an average of only $55 per week on his product. Then the burgeoning aerospace industry discovered VELCRO® brand fasteners. Aircraft engineers began using them to fasten or secure various parts of their planes, from insulation to seat panels. At the end of the 1950s, more than sixty million yards of VELCRO® brand fasteners were being produced annually.

The word "Velcro" derives from the French words *velours* (velvet) and *crochet* (hook).

Still, Velcro Industries' big break did not come until the 1960s, when the National Aeronautics and Space Administration (NASA) began sending rockets into outer space. NASA engineers used VELCRO® brand fasteners to secure items in zero-gravity environments. Images of space travel caught the public imagination and introduced the fastener to mainstream America. Indeed, many people mistakenly believed VELCRO® brand fasteners had been designed by NASA.

Even after selling his Swiss company, de Mestral continued to earn royalties from his invention, estimated to be in the millions. He also continued to invent—a pillbox designed to help organize daily medications, a device for measuring humidity, and a commercially successful asparagus peeler. Mainly, de Mestral dedicated himself to inspiring and supporting other, often younger, inventors. He died on February 8, 1990, in Commugny, Switzerland.

Almost a decade after his death, de Mestral was inducted into the Inventors Hall of Fame for his creation. At the event in 1999 he was represented by his son, who said, "He believed that what mattered most was not the money he received for his work, but the esteem he received from his contemporaries."

"Velcro" is the name of a set of companies called Velcro Industries B.V. The company is not without competition. Copycat

The Pull of Mother Nature

Burrs like these inspired de Mestral to create his product.

The hook-and-loop fastener is revolutionary for reasons far beyond its strength and **durability**. It is often recalled as the first real instance of **biomimetics**.

The burrs that inspired de Mestral had evolved as a means of pollination—the hooks ensured that the plant seeds contained within the burr could be spread far and wide. The burr design had secured the success of the plant species for eons. De Mestral recognized the potential of the hook-and-loop design and successfully duplicated it with VELCRO® brand fasteners. Little did he know that, decades later, an entire academic discipline would spring up around this very act.

products sprang up even before the original patent expired in 1979. Now, other companies, such as Japanese manufacturer YKK and American company W.L. Gore & Associates, manufacture hook-and-loop fasteners.

Since its creation, the VELCRO® brand fastener has become a useful aspect of society. They are popular on children's shoes, sporting equipment, and high-end fashion. Today, both the aerospace and automobile industries use them on their products, including astronauts' suits and car seat covers. The medical industry has also benefitted from using VELCRO® brand fasteners. They were involved in the first artificial heart surgery and have been used to close wounds. Their impact on society has been immense, and continue to be used in surprising and innovative ways.

*VELCRO® is a registered trademark of Velcro Industries B.V.

Timeline

1907
George de Mestral born in Lausanne, Switzerland

1941
De Mestral is inspired to create hook-and-loop fasteners during a walk in the mountains

1952
De Mestral founds Velcro S.A.

1958
The US branch of de Mestral's company opens in Manchester, New Hampshire

1960s
NASA's use of hook-and-loop fasteners vastly increases the popularity of de Mestral's invention

1979
De Mestral's patent expires, opening the door to competitors

1990
De Mestral dies in Switzerland

1999
De Mestral is posthumously inducted into the Inventors Hall of Fame

James Dyson

1947–

Not all inventors must create new products that change the world. Some inventors build on already existing machines. However, improving inventions already in use can be tricky. British engineer James Dyson discovered this while reinventing a new kind of household product: the vacuum cleaner. With its introduction in the nineteenth century, the vacuum cleaner changed the way society functioned and improved household cleaning. By the twentieth century, a different take on the invention was not necessarily needed; however, Dyson had plans for a new, modern, and more efficient kind of vacuum cleaner. Eventually, his idea would find success in the marketplace, but it took much effort and a lot of determination before it was accepted.

A Builder's Beginnings

James Dyson

A child of academic parents, James Dyson was born in 1947 and grew up in Norfolk in eastern England. He never intended to be an inventor. At school, he took no science courses. Rather, his interests focused on art and design. At age nineteen, he began studying furniture design and interior design at London's Royal College of Art (RCA). Then, something unexpected happened. "While at the RCA, I accidentally discovered the glories of making things," Dyson recalled later. "And I can tell you it was quite a shock when I realized I was getting interested in engineering."

In the late 1960s, Dyson designed theaters, airport lounges, and wine shops before focusing on inventing. Working with British inventor Jeremy Fry, he developed a fast military boat, the Sea Truck, which won awards and sold in fifty countries. By 1970, he was working at Fry's company, Rotork, managing the Sea Truck project.

Shortly thereafter, Dyson set up a firm to develop his own ideas. His first big invention, in 1974, was the Ballbarrow: a wheelbarrow with a large red ball at the front instead of a wheel. This ball made it much more maneuverable over muddy ground than a traditional barrow. Later, he used the same idea to make the Trolleyball, a boat-launching trolley with balls instead of wheels. The Waterolla was another invention from this period. It was a simple garden roller (a device for flattening rough ground) that had in place of the usual metal roller a large plastic cylinder that could be filled with water, turning it into a heavy rolling drum.

Defining the Problem

In 1979, at age thirty-two, Dyson bought and started renovating an old country house and was irritated when his secondhand vacuum cleaner became clogged with dust. He discovered a similar problem at his Ballbarrow factory, where the air filter was constantly blocked with powder from the manufacturing process. Dyson designed a new machine that would clean the air by sucking in dusty air, spinning it around to remove the dust using **centrifugal force**, and then blowing clean air back into the room.

Dyson was delighted with this machine and began to wonder why the same technique was not used in domestic vacuums. So he started tinkering with a cereal box and some masking tape, and he built a model of a centrifugal vacuum cleaner. Between 1979 and 1984, he tried no fewer than 5,127 different prototypes of his invention until he had a product he could manufacture. During this time, he searched Europe in vain for investors who would finance the project, but he could not convince anyone that customers wanted vacuum cleaners to work any differently. With no luck in Europe, he took his product to Japan. Named the G-Force, it was manufactured there from 1986 and became a great success. This original model was bright pink and became a status symbol in Japan, selling for $2,000.

Designing the Solution

Dyson, however, was determined to make a product that he could sell more widely. In 1993, using money he had earned from the G-Force, he started manufacturing a new model, the Dyson DC01, in his own British factory. Even though the DC01 cost twice as much as a conventional vacuum, it had twice the suction of a normal vacuum with no messy bags to change. The DC01 became the best-selling vacuum in Britain within two years. Dyson was quickly seen as more than an inventor. In Britain, he became a national hero: he was making a successful product in his own country at a time when it seemed virtually all domestic appliances were being manufactured overseas and imported.

Applying the Solution

Throughout the 1990s, sales continued to rise. Dyson's products earned design awards worldwide, and he received many personal honors, including being named a Commander of the British Empire, one of Britain's highest awards. He also encountered difficulties. In 1997, he brought a case before the European Court of Human Rights to protest patent fees that inventors have to pay to protect their ideas. He also won lawsuits against the Hoover and Electrolux companies, which he claimed had copied parts of his invention and infringed on his patent.

As Dyson's reputation grew, the value of the Dyson brand also grew—and he used it to sell new inventions. In 2000, he launched a washing machine called the DC06 Contrarotator that had two different drums rotating in opposite directions. The same year, he began selling a revolutionary carpet cleaner, the DC04 Zorbster. Both products won awards.

As part of his plan to conquer the American market, he announced he would close his British factory and relocate manufacturing to Malaysia. The outraged British media claimed that eight hundred assembly-line jobs would be lost, but Dyson defended the decision robustly: "All our competitors were manufacturing in China, while we were watching our profits go into free fall. I could see our demise." In the end, he was able to save 210 of the 800 jobs by expanding his British research and development wing. The decision to manufacture overseas was controversial, but it was vindicated by the continuing success of Dyson's company.

The Dyson Company continues to produce new products each year. The DC37 (pictured here) was introduced in 2011.

Inventors of Everyday Technology

The Impact of the Solution on Society

Today, Dyson and his vacuum cleaners continue to have success in the marketplace. He has different lines of various devices—upright, handheld, and cordless. His products do well around the world, selling £1 billion ($151,7625,000) as of 2012, with particular popularity in the US and Japan. To show his appreciation for other aspiring inventors, James Dyson has started the James Dyson Award, an international award granted to "a current or recent design engineering student" who shows much promise for the future of invention. It is Dyson's wish to "inspire the next generation of design students and design engineers." Overall, Dyson and his revolutionizing device illustrated that not all inventions must be fresh creations, but that with reinventing an existing concept, a more improved model can also influence society.

Timeline

1947
James Dyson born in Norfolk, England

1960s
Dyson develops the Sea Truck with Jeremy Fry

1974
Dyson invents the Ballbarrow

1979
Dyson begins work on a new type of vacuum cleaner

1986
Dyson launches the G-Force vacuum cleaner in Japan

1993
Dyson begins manufacturing the Dyson DC01 in Britain

2000
Dyson launches a washing machine and carpet cleaner

George
Eastman

1854–1932

Throughout history, inventors and their inventions demonstrate new ways of viewing the world, of visualizing concepts, or of improving lifestyle practices. Many inventors begin as scientists or technicians; however, this is not always the case. George Eastman, for example, was firstly and mostly a businessman. His story follows a different yet influential path to success. He began his inventing years in business and continued to view creations with a business eye. Along the way, he created a recognizable organization—the Eastman Kodak Company—that still exists today. While he may be most known for his shrewd business sense and the company that bore his name, he also took a concept once for the privileged few and transformed it into an accessible product for everyday use.

Tough Beginnings

George Eastman

George Eastman was born in 1854 in Waterville, New York, the youngest of three children. His father, George Washington Eastman, owned a business school in Rochester, New York, about 120 miles (193 kilometers) from Waterville. In the 1860s, the Eastman family moved to Rochester, where they lived well. In 1862, however, Eastman's father became ill and died, and Eastman's mother, Maria, had to take in boarders to make ends meet.

In 1868, Eastman dropped out of school over his mother's objections to contribute financially to the family. Life continued to be difficult for the Eastman family, and George's polio-stricken older sister died in 1870. Following her death, George Eastman worked his way up to better-paying jobs, becoming an insurance agent and then a bank clerk.

Defining the Problem

In 1877, while Eastman was working as a bookkeeper, he heard about a real estate boom in the Caribbean. He considered visiting there to invest in real estate, and a friend suggested that he learn photography—a budding art form—so he could make a record of potential sites. Eastman never made the trip, but he did pay nearly $50 (a large amount at a time when the average annual salary was between $300 and $400) for photographic gear, or an "outfit," as it was known at the time. The massive size and weight of the outfit troubled him; he later recalled thinking that "it seemed that one ought to be able to carry less than a packhorse load" when taking pictures.

Creating a photograph in the nineteenth century was a major undertaking. Just to take a picture, a photographer had to take a sheet (also known as a plate) of glass, dip it into egg whites, coat it with a variety of chemicals (called an emulsion) to make it sensitive to light, and then load the glass into a camera. Once the photograph was taken, the photographer had to develop it. The process of developing a photograph was so complicated that almost the only people who took the trouble to learn it were those planning to make a living as photographers.

Eastman, who was interested in taking outdoor photographs, faced another complication: the emulsion had to be put on the glass plates in the dark to avoid overexposure. Consequently, whenever Eastman wanted to take a photograph outside, he first had to set up a dark tent in which he could prepare his plates.

In 1878, Eastman became interested in a new tool, a dry-emulsion plate, which he had read about in a photography journal. Unlike the wet-emulsion plates he was using, a dry-emulsion plate could be prepared ahead of time and loaded into a camera at the photographer's convenience. Eastman quickly set out to make his own dry-emulsion plates. "At first," he later recalled, "I wanted to make photography simpler merely for my own convenience, but soon I thought of the possibilities of commercial production."

Designing the Solution

Eastman was not the only one who saw the commercial potential of dry-emulsion plates, which soon began to appear in stores. The plates were made by hand and were relatively expensive; Eastman thought that a machine could be used to make them less expensively. In 1879, Eastman took a leave of absence from his work and traveled to London, where he patented a machine for producing dry-emulsion plates. Eastman returned to the United States, where he patented the machine again and set up a factory to produce dry-emulsion plates. He began manufacturing Eastman-brand plates for sale while keeping his bookkeeping job.

In 1881, Eastman quit his job and began to focus on his plate business full-time. That year, he also began looking for a substitute for the heavy, breakable glass plates used to make negatives. He created a workable film using coated paper that had been treated with oil to make it transparent. In 1885, along with another photographer, Eastman developed a "roll holder" that allowed users to convert their plate cameras to ones that could use paper film.

At the time, these products did not appeal to serious photographers. Despite all the inconveniences of the traditional camera, prints made from glass plates were crisper and more detailed than ones made from paper film. Eastman realized that he was not going to convert professional photographers to his film; instead, the key to enlarging his business would be to expand the popularity of photography by making it accessible to more people.

In 1888, Eastman introduced a new camera to the market, one that was remarkable in its simplicity: the Kodak. While not cheap, the Kodak was relatively inexpensive for a camera, costing $25. So small that it did not require a tripod and could be held in the hand or worn around the neck with a strap, it came preloaded with enough paper film to take one hundred photographs. Once the film was used up, the customer could mail the entire camera back to the Kodak plant, which for $10 would develop all the pictures and reload the camera with fresh film.

The name "Kodak" was devised by Eastman, who wanted a short, distinctive name for his camera that would be easy to pronounce and would contain the letter k, which he liked. Eastman also devised a popular slogan touting the simplicity of his camera: "You press the button, we do the rest."

Applying the Solution

The camera caused a sensation, swiftly opening the field of photography to anyone who could push a button to take a picture. Within eight years, about one hundred thousand Kodaks were sold, a remarkable feat for a camera in the late nineteenth century. Kodak cameras began to show up in unexpected locales, with enthusiastic amateurs snapping pictures of people on the street or at the beach—sometimes to the dismay of those being photographed. Numerous magazine and newspaper articles were written about the Kodak craze and those "kodakers" who had been swept up in it, and the name "Kodak" appeared in popular songs and musicals.

Some predicted that the handheld camera craze would be replaced by another fad, but Eastman was more optimistic. He observed that people were not taking photographs simply for the sake of recreation;

they were taking photographs to record events in their lives, a need that would not disappear.

Under Eastman's leadership, what eventually became the Eastman Kodak Company continued to develop smaller, cheaper, easier-to-use cameras, eventually creating a $1 camera with 15-cent film—the Brownie. That camera, introduced in 1900, was marketed specifically to children, in keeping with Eastman's philosophy that cameras could be made simple enough for anyone to use.

The Impact of the Solution on Society

Although paper film was lighter and less fragile than glass plates, it was far from perfect. Paper had a grain that appeared in prints, and paper film was delicate. Eastman realized that the film market could become lucrative, as film was used once and replaced often.

As early as 1888, Eastman made it a priority to develop a tough, flexible, transparent film. The next year, one of Eastman's chemists, Henry Reichenbach, made a breakthrough, creating a workable film out of celluloid, a durable yet flexible material made from plant fiber. By August 1889, Eastman had the film on the market, and within months it was selling so well that the company could not produce the film fast enough.

Eastman kept on top of film technology, creating film products for X-rays after their discovery in 1895. In 1889, Eastman developed film for motion pictures, then produced a fireproof safety film in 1909.

By the early twentieth century, Eastman Kodak employed around four thousand people and had operations in Europe, North America, and Asia. The company would eventually come to control more than three-quarters of the total photography business in the United States. Eastman continued to run Eastman Kodak before semi-retiring in 1925. By then, he had begun to move away from laboratory work to focus on managing his increasingly massive firm.

Nonetheless, Eastman continued to recognize the importance of research to the success of his company. He recognized, too, that increased accessibility to technical and scientific education would benefit the photography industry. Eastman, one of the wealthiest people in the United States by the early twentieth century, became a major philanthropist, ultimately donating $80 million to various institutions. Among those donations were major gifts to the University of Rochester, the Tuskegee Normal and Industrial Institute, and the Massachusetts Institute of Technology, which was able to build an entire campus because of Eastman's generosity.

Eastman enjoyed donating the money and planning how that money would be used. "Men who leave their money to be distributed by others [after they die] are pie-faced mutts," he once declared. "I want to see the action during my lifetime."

During the late 1920s and early 1930s, however, Eastman's health declined. By 1932, he was unable to go to the office or travel, he was often in pain, and his staff tried to protect him by discouraging visitors. Eastman reportedly became isolated and depressed, feeling that he had nothing left to contribute and nothing to look forward to.

More than a Name

Eastman School of Music in Rochester, New York

George Eastman was known for more than just his company. In Rochester, New York, the Eastman name is also given to the Eastman School of Music, a prestigious college of music, and the University of Rochester's Eastman Dental Center. It was Eastman's last request that the money he left behind be used to encourage people to pursue education, appreciate the arts, and expand medical services in the local community. In the town where George Eastman established a photographic empire, his legacy and influence live on today.

On March 14, 1932, at the age of seventy-seven, Eastman committed suicide by shooting himself in the heart.

The Eastman Kodak Company survived its founder's death; however, in 2012, the company—now just known as Kodak—filed for bankruptcy. In 2013, its digital patents were sold to competitors Google and Apple. Although reeling from its recent difficulties, Kodak still exists, though it is no longer the dominating force of the industry. With the advent of digital photography, computer, software, and even telephone companies have entered the field of photography, challenging the once giant corporation.

Regardless, Eastman's vision for a new type of photography became a reality that revolutionized society. It made photographs more accessible and encouraged new ways of thinking about a more digital civilization. With his innovation, Eastman made photography a popular and successful pastime, one that continues to exist today.

Timeline

1854
George Eastman born in Waterville, New York

1878
Eastman becomes interested in photography

1879
Eastman patents a machine to produce dry emulsion plates

1881
Eastman invents photographic film

1885
Eastman develops the roll holder

1888
Eastman introduces the Kodak camera

1900
The Brownie is released

1932
Eastman dies

Thomas Edison

1847–1931

Every so often, a person with the ability to invent many different devices within his or her lifetime appears. A few examples include Leonardo da Vinci, Benjamin Franklin, and Beulah Henry. A contemporary of Henry's is another of the great inventors to add to this list, Thomas Edison. Edison conceptualized different inventions that grew to have a profound effect on society. From the lightbulb to moviemaking, Edison's contributions to the world of inventions are still known and cherished today. Without inventions like Edison's, the world would be a very different place.

Edison's Beginnings

Edison was born on February 11, 1847, in the Great Lakes port town of Milan, Ohio; he was the last of seven children of Samuel Ogden Edison and Nancy Matthews Elliott, his wife. When Edison was seven, the family moved to Port Huron, Michigan, where his father became a grain merchant. Edison began school in Port Huron—an education lasting just twelve weeks.

Thomas Edison and his phonograph ca. 1878

From an early age, Edison had difficulty hearing. At the time, most learning was by **rote**. Edison's hearing problem made this impossible in a class full of noisy young children. His teacher, a minister named Engle, branded him a misfit. Observing that Edison's head was large and strangely shaped, Engle suggested that the boy's brains were "addled" and defective.

Edison's mother, a former schoolteacher, decided to teach him at home. Edison later wrote: "My mother was the making of me. She was so true, so sure of me; and I felt I had something to live for, someone I must not disappoint." His mother gave him a love of learning, and he eagerly read everything from science books to Shakespeare's plays, from poetry to world history.

Edison's father was reasonably wealthy, and as a young boy Edison did not need to work. However, he wanted independence. In 1859, he took a job selling newspapers and candy on trains that ran on the Grand Trunk Railroad. Three years later, at age fifteen, he started compiling his own weekly newspaper, printing it on a small handpress in the baggage car and selling it on the train. This gave Edison a taste of fame: England's newspaper, the *Times*, reported the venture as the first newspaper ever to be printed on a moving train.

Defining the Problem

One day, while selling papers on the train, Edison saved a boy's life. The child's grateful father, who worked at the train station, rewarded Edison by teaching him how to operate a telegraph. This invention used electric cables to carry messages back and forth at high speed, one letter at a time, written in Morse code, a special pattern of short (dots) and long (dashes) electrical pulses. Learning about the telegraph changed Edison's life. In 1862, he started working as a telegraph operator in a bookstore in Port Huron. The following year, he operated telegraphs along the Grand Trunk Railroad in Ontario, Canada, before returning to the United States.

Over the next five years, Edison worked his way from one telegraph office to another. This experience gave him an idea for his first invention, the automatic telegraph repeater. It could carry messages in Morse code through unmanned offices to stations farther down the line. Despite the usefulness of the invention, Edison was reprimanded by his boss, who believed the young inventor was wasting company time.

"Opportunity is missed by most people because it is dressed in overalls and looks like work."
—Thomas Edison

Edison moved to Boston in 1868 and to New York City the following year. In New York, at age twenty-one, he invented an electric machine that could count votes in elections. Unfortunately, that invention never took off, but Edison's flair for inventing soon earned him rewards. While working for a financial company, he was asked to improve its "stock ticker"—a printer that recorded stock prices arriving as telegraph messages—and was paid a large sum.

Edison made many improvements to the telegraph in the 1870s, and he set up several companies to implement them. One of his greatest achievements was devising a method to send four different messages along a single telegraph wire concurrently. He called this invention the "quadruplex telegraph" and sold it to Jay Gould, American businessman and so-called **robber baron**, for $30,000 (about $552,000 US in 2014). This achievement marked Edison's arrival as a successful inventor.

On Christmas Day 1871, Edison married Mary Stilwell, a woman who had worked for one his companies. They had three children; the first two, Marion and Thomas Jr., he affectionately nicknamed "Dot" and "Dash."

Designing the Solution

In 1876, Edison used his money from the telegraph to set up a research laboratory at Menlo Park, New Jersey, where he developed some of his greatest inventions. Edison's laboratory was a messy, creative place with no rules—dirt was allowed to gather on the floor, workers could spit freely, and a chained-up pet bear stood guard outside (until it broke free in April 1877 and had to be killed).

Later that year, a company called Western Union persuaded Edison to develop a new telephone that could compete with the one that Alexander Graham Bell had invented. Soon, Edison developed a carbon

A Revoluntionary Invention

When the phonograph was first demonstrated, Edison's employees could not believe what they were hearing. Some thought it was a magic trick; others insisted there was a ventriloquist hiding in the room, making the sounds. Either way, it seemed unbelievable: as they huddled around the little machine, one day in 1877, they distinctly heard Edison's voice crackling out of the horn: "Mary had a little lamb, its fleece was white as snow." This "little piece of practical poetry," as Edison called it, was the world's first sound recording. The machine that stored the sound and played it back was Edison's phonograph, the ancestor of every modern sound recording technology, from the vinyl record and the magnetic cassette to the sampling keyboard and the iPod.

Edison did not originally see the phonograph as a way of storing and playing back music. He imagined people would use phonographs in their homes, as telephone answering machines, or in offices, as aids to dictation. Another early use he imagined was in toys. He

Inventors of Everyday Technology

microphone that captured sound more clearly than Bell's. During this research, Edison found he needed a way to signal the beginning of a telephone conversation to someone at the other end of the line and hit upon "Hello"—another of his inventions that became universal.

Edison's telephone work led to another breakthrough later the same year. He had already developed machines to help telegraph operators record incoming messages; now he wondered if he could produce something similar for the telephone. This led him to invent the phonograph, the world's first sound-recording machine. The phonograph secured Edison's fame.

A reporter from a newspaper, the *New York Graphic*, came to interview Edison at Menlo Park and commented: "Aren't you a good deal of a wizard, Mr. Edison?" When the paper ran the interview, it carried a picture of Edison wearing a wizard's hat on its front cover, and his nickname, "the wizard of Menlo Park," was born.

If the phonograph proved that Edison could be original, his next invention demonstrated his more practical side. During 1878 and

formed a company to manufacture talking dolls with windup speaking cylinders inside them, which could automatically recite nursery rhymes. The phonograph was not an immediate success, however, and Edison lost interest in the idea for almost a decade while he devoted himself to electric light and power.

Returning to the idea in 1887, he developed an improved phonograph using wax cylinders instead of foil sheets. During the 1890s, Edison released a whole series of improved phonographs, with a standard model costing around $20 (about $528 US in 2014). In the early 1900s, his companies began selling mass-produced wax cylinders, each capable of storing two to four minutes of prerecorded sound or music, and costing from 50 cents ($13.20 US in 2014) to $4 ($106 US in 2014).

Edison's rivals initially copied his idea, but they later switched to flat circular discs that could be played on a similar machine called a gramophone. When in 1912 Edison started selling his own version, the disc phonograph, the days of the cylinder phonograph were numbered.

1879, after filling forty thousand pages of notes with scribbled ideas, Edison developed an improved electric lightbulb. It consisted of a thin piece of material (called filament) that glowed red hot and gave off light when electricity passed through it. Earlier light designs had worked in a similar manner, but their carbon filaments quickly burned up in the air, so they were never practical. To find the perfect filament, Edison experimented with more than six thousand different materials, including cotton, bamboo gathered specifically for that purpose in Japan, and even red hair, before settling on wire made from tungsten metal. Edison also placed his filament inside a glass vacuum bulb, extending its life by hundreds of times. Although Edison did not invent the electric light, he turned it into the practical invention that lit up people's homes.

From 1878 onward, Edison moved to capitalize on electricity: his idea was to sell electric light to the nation and later to the world. However, before he could do so, he had to provide people with electric power. Thus, he began designing dynamos (coal-powered electricity generators). He nicknamed his first one "Long-Legged Mary Ann," in honor of its two tall magnets, which stood upright like a gigantic pair of legs. Machines like these formed the heart of the world's earliest power plants, which Edison built during the 1880s. He opened the first of these on Pearl Street, in New York City, on September 4, 1882, supplying electricity to fifty-nine customers in lower Manhattan.

Applying the Solution

With his work now centered on New York City, Edison closed his Menlo Park laboratory. Working from offices at 65 Fifth Avenue, he maintained a feverish pace. In 1882, he applied for 141 patents (an average of two to three a week), just over half of which were eventually granted. Some days he worked eighteen or nineteen hours, unaware of whether it was day or night, stopping to eat only when he was hungry—and spending hardly any time with his wife and family. He once said, "I owe my success to the fact that I never had a clock in my workroom."

Still only in his mid-thirties, Edison was securing his reputation as a great inventor and the father of the electrical age. In 1884,

Edison's wife, Mary, died of typhoid fever, leaving him to bring up three small children. Two years later, he married Mina Miller; they had three children, including Charles—who as an adult would run his father's businesses and be elected governor of New Jersey. Edison acquired a large estate, Glenmont, in West Orange, New Jersey, for his expanding family and, in 1887, built himself a huge new research laboratory—or "invention factory," as he called it—nearby.

West Orange marked a turning point in Edison's life. At Menlo Park, he had worked with a small team on a few ideas. However, at West Orange, more inventions were in development and more people were involved. Edison was also increasingly moving from the role of inventor to industrialist: he was no longer merely thinking of ideas but was now running companies to profit from them. The West Orange lab was a more businesslike place than Menlo Park. It was run by managers and administrators, workers had to punch a time clock, and Edison became more aloof, directing the lab rather than working in it himself.

During this period, Edison began to experience some serious commercial failures. In 1887, he developed a way of using electricity and magnetism to separate gold and iron from their ores (rocks dug from the ground). He spent more than a decade and a large amount of money on this project, bought 145 old mines, and developed a gigantic and hugely expensive plant in New Jersey. Although he expected to make a fortune, he never perfected the process and was forced to close the plant in the 1890s at a loss of $2 million. Edison experienced another major disappointment around the same time when the system he used for supplying electric power—known as direct current—was shown to be inferior to a rival system, alternating current, promoted by the Westinghouse Electrical Company.

While trying to think of ways to promote the phonograph, Edison hit upon his next big idea: the movie camera and projector. In the 1880s, he had seen demonstrations of toys that could make images appear to move. They worked by spinning a series of still pictures on a wheel until the images blurred together in the viewer's eye to make a moving scene. With his assistant William Dickson (1860–1935), Edison developed an invention that took this idea a step further. It was a primitive movie camera called the kinetograph that could record a series of still photographs on to a length of celluloid film. The same filmstrip could later be run at high speed through a piece of apparatus called a kinetoscope so people could view the "movie."

In 1893, Edison opened the world's first studio, nicknamed the "Black Maria," and began filming short motion pictures. Because the concept of the movie theater had not yet been brought to realization, Edison's movies could be viewed by only one person at a time. Viewers had to peer inside coin-operated kinetoscopes in large parlors where dozens of machines were installed side by side. Soon after, two French brothers, Auguste and Louis Lumière (1862–1954; 1864–1948), saw some of Edison's machines. When they figured out

Rivals of Invention

Photo. Barraud.
NICOLA TESLA.

Nikola Tesla became one of Thomas Edison's biggest rivals.

Edison's brilliance made him many friends, such as Henry Ford, Marie Curie, Herbert Hoover, and Charles Lindbergh. It made him enemies, too, none more so than Croatian-born inventor Nikola Tesla (1856–1943). Tesla settled in New York City in 1884, where he was employed by Edison, who was busy bringing electricity to the nation. However, the two men could not get along, so Tesla quit the following year and struck out alone.

Edison and Tesla were prolific inventors (Tesla eventually gained one hundred patents from a total of around seven hundred different inventions) and visionaries who could see that electricity would power the future. Yet they were also bitter rivals who disagreed on a fundamental issue. Edison believed in a type of power called direct current (DC), in which electricity moves continually in the same direction.

how to make a better camera that could project images onto a wall, modern movies were born.

The Impact of the Solution on Society

Much of Edison's time was devoted to developing three ideas: electric light and power, sound recording, and movies. However, he still found time to explore other ideas. In the 1880s and 1890s, he developed large electric batteries. He originally designed these to help his friend Henry Ford (1863–1947), the automobile pioneer, who wanted to use electricity in his cars. Edison and Ford dreamed of using batteries to make an electric-powered car, but their creations never succeeded in

Tesla thought alternating current (AC) was better. In this system, the electric current reverses direction (alternates) many times each second. The advantage of alternating current is that it can be transformed (boosted electrically) to a much higher voltage and then be carried many miles from a power station to where it is needed with much less loss of power than with direct current.

After leaving Edison's firm, Tesla worked by himself to develop his AC power system, completing its design around 1887. The following year, he sold the rights to the Westinghouse Electrical Company. Edison did his best to fight the AC system with canny publicity stunts. For example, he actively campaigned for the death penalty to be administered by an AC-powered electric chair because he thought this would convince people that AC was a lethal technology. As part of his battle, he staged outrageous demonstrations for the press: he killed cats, dogs, a horse, and even an elephant called Topsy to demonstrate the dangers of AC electricity—leading the press to coin a new word, "electrocution."

Edison won the publicity battle, but Westinghouse won the war. It was awarded the contract to build a giant power plant at Niagara Falls using Tesla's AC system in the 1890s, defeating a rival bid from Edison's DC system. Since then, virtually all of the world's electric power has been supplied using AC.

rivaling the gasoline engine. In 1910, Edison demonstrated a way of making a home from poured concrete, receiving great acclaim.

During World War I, when a journalist asked Edison how the United States could win wars, he suggested that the US government "should maintain a great research laboratory" like his own. In 1915, the government asked Edison to head the Naval Consulting Board, a body that would advise the navy on using the latest technology. During this period, Edison made many discoveries helpful to the military, including a new way of launching torpedoes and a method of manufacturing synthetic rubber (to avoid being dependent on imports of natural rubber during the war). In 1923, Edison's work led Congress to set up the Naval Research Laboratory, which has remained one of the world's most important centers of military innovation.

Edison remained active well into his seventies, and his pace of work slowed only when his health began to fail. When he resigned as president of his company in 1926, his son Charles took over. Edison filed his last patent application on January 6, 1931, and died in West Orange nine months later on October 18. Just before his death, he woke briefly from a coma and uttered his last words to his wife: "It is very beautiful over there." A few days later, every electric light in the country—including the one that powered the torch in the Statue of Liberty—was turned off for one minute in tribute.

Edison's inventions had a huge impact on people's lives. More than any other individual, he helped to usher in the modern age of electric power, convenience, and entertainment. His filament light demonstrated the usefulness of electricity, opened the door to electric power, and encouraged others to develop more electrical appliances. While Edison's electricity changed homes and businesses, his work on sound recording and the movies improved people's social lives, and his telegraph and telephone improvements brought advances in communication.

Although Edison's inventions were often technical, he was more of a hands-on experimenter than a scientist or theoretician. He made no secret of this: "I try an experiment and reason out the result, somehow, by methods which I could not explain." Driven by the old saying that "necessity is the mother of invention," he always ensured that his inventions met people's needs, and he continued to perfect his inventions long after they had been launched. All this required immense perseverance, a trait he acquired during the early years when his mother had encouraged him to overcome his hearing disability with hard work. Indeed, his most famous saying was, "Genius is 1 percent inspiration and 99 percent perspiration."

For his achievements and contributions to the world of invention, Thomas Edison will be remembered. His improvements to inventions such as electricity and the lightbulb presented new ideas to an eager society. He challenged ways of thinking and although he did not always come out the victor, Thomas Edison has remained a profound figure in history. To this day, he is still known and studied with admiration and appreciation.

Timeline

1847
Thomas Edison born in Milan, Ohio

1862
Edison begins work as a telegraph operator

1870s
Edison makes several improvements to the telegraph

1876
Edison sets up a research laboratory in Menlo Park, New Jersey

1877
Edison invents the carbon microphone and phonograph

1879
Edison invents the electric lightbulb

1882
Edison opens the first electric power plant in New York City

1893
Edison opens the first movie studio

1926
Edison resigns as president of his company

1931
Edison files his last patent application and dies later that year

Daniel Fahrenheit

1686–1736

After looking outside on a cold day, many people consult a thermometer. If they live in the United States, they read the temperature by degrees Fahrenheit. The term "Fahrenheit" is most commonly known as a measurement today, but it was once also the name of the person who gave the measurement its name. Daniel Fahrenheit was a scientist living in the eighteenth century who developed a temperature-reading measurement and a scale for calculating that number. Likewise, he developed the first mercury thermometer—which is still used today—and demonstrated how boiling-point temperatures vary with **atmospheric pressure**. For his contributions to society, Daniel Fahrenheit is remembered and celebrated as a great inventor of his time.

An Inventor Is Born

Daniel Fahrenheit

Daniel Gabriel Fahrenheit was born into a well-to-do household in Danzig (modern-day Gdansk, Poland) on May 14, 1686, the eldest of five children. His father was a merchant. Both his parents died on the same day in 1701; it is thought that they ate poisonous mushrooms. His four younger siblings were placed in foster homes, but Daniel Fahrenheit, then fifteen, was apprenticed to a merchant in Amsterdam, the Netherlands, to train as a bookkeeper. There Fahrenheit became interested in scientific instruments. After his apprenticeship, he abandoned bookkeeping and worked as a glassblower.

Interested in expanding his knowledge of scientific instrumentation, Fahrenheit began to travel sometime in 1707. He wandered extensively across northern Europe, seeking out scientists and instrument makers in Denmark, Poland, Germany, and Sweden, as well as in England.

Defining the Problem

Many scientists throughout the seventeenth century and the early eighteenth century experimented with instruments capable of measuring temperature. The great expansion of scientific inquiry in this period led many to devise such tools as part of a larger interest in measuring and quantifying all natural phenomena. Variations among the many types of thermometers of the time, however, made it impossible to refer to a common measure of air temperature.

During the 1720s, Fahrenheit had been constructing and working with different kinds of thermometers. Those of the time normally used a combination of water and alcohol and were better than the gas (air) thermometers that had been in use since the early 1600s. However, they were still inaccurate.

One of the scientists Fahrenheit met on his travels was the Danish astronomer Olaus Roemer (1644–1719). Roemer had invented a

Eighteenth-century
thermometer

thermometer that used alcohol to measure temperature. Alcohol was
preferred to water because, when sealed inside the glass, it was less
susceptible to changes in atmospheric pressure. By 1714, Fahrenheit
had constructed his first thermometers. That year, he demonstrated
two of them: both contained alcohol, and they gave identical air
temperatures—the first time such a feat had been accomplished.

Also in 1714, Fahrenheit devised the first mercury thermometer.
He used mercury because it expanded at a much more constant and
predictable rate than either alcohol or water and could be used to

measure a wider range of temperatures. Sealed inside newly improved glass tubing, Fahrenheit's mercury remained unaffected by changes in air pressure. With this significantly more stable instrument for measuring and recording the temperature of substances, Fahrenheit set about creating a standard scale that could be used by people in different places.

Designing the Solution

At the time, many different techniques and scales were applied for making basic observations about air temperature. Comparing the temperature in Amsterdam with the temperature in London was impossible without a common method of calculation. After meeting with Roemer in Denmark, Fahrenheit saw the need to base his system on two fixed points.

Roemer had been the first to introduce this idea. He had chosen as his upper point the boiling point of water (which he labeled 60) and as his lower point the melting point of ice (which he labeled 7.5). What

The Thermometer Is Born

Although Fahrenheit is considered the inventor of the modern thermometer, instruments for measuring heat or cold, in fact, go back many years earlier. Galileo Galilei (1564–1642) was one of the first to develop an instrument to measure the expansion or contraction of air inside a glass container.

Around 1600, Galileo poured water through an opening in a long, narrow glass tube connected to a glass bulb. As the air under the water expanded (warmed) the water would rise; and as it contracted (cooled), the water level would lower. Water, however, did not provide very accurate readings because it was so easily affected by changes in atmospheric pressure. Called a thermoscope, Galileo's instrument had no means of measuring temperature, so it was not a proper thermometer. In 1612, an Italian inventor, Santorio Santorio (1561–1636), applied a scale to a glass tube similar to the one Galileo used, thereby allowing the measurement and recording of temperature.

Roemer had not realized was that the boiling point of water varied with atmospheric pressure—a relationship that Fahrenheit was the first to comprehend. The effect of pressure on boiling points is observable on a mountaintop, where the pressure is lower than at sea level; water at higher altitudes boils at a lower temperature.

Wanting to base his system on more commonly occurring temperatures, Fahrenheit chose the temperature of the human body as his upper point (which he originally set at 96) and the temperature of a mixture of salt, water, and ice (0 degrees) as his lower point. He then divided his system into 96 equal parts and established the freezing point of water at 32 degrees. Later, the boiling point of water was calibrated to be 212 degrees.

Applying the Solution

Fahrenheit continued working in Amsterdam from 1717 until his death in 1736. In 1724 he published his only account of his methods

Inventing the Fahrenheit Scale

After Daniel Fahrenheit invented a mercury thermometer capable of more consistent temperature readings, he established a scale that could be used everywhere so that people could refer to a common number for a given temperature—including the boiling and freezing points of water. Many have wondered why Fahrenheit chose 32 degrees as the number for freezing and 212 for boiling.

Early on, Fahrenheit had been influenced by Olaus Roemer, who had established fixed points for the boiling point of water and the melting point of ice, which he labeled 60 degrees and 7.5 degrees, respectively. Fahrenheit based his own thermometer scale on Roemer's principles, but with some crucial changes. First, he did not want to work with "inconvenient and awkward fractions." Second, since Fahrenheit was primarily interested in measuring real atmospheric temperatures, he did not concern himself with the boiling point of water. A thermometer that would record temperatures that high was of no use in meteorology.

in the *Philosophical Transactions of the Royal Society* in London, which elected him to membership that same year.

The success of Fahrenheit's thermometer and his way of measuring temperature took some time to develop, and over time, many people made adjustments to these inventions. Today, however, thermometers are used in places such as hospitals, veterinary clinics, and weather stations. Likewise, degrees Fahrenheit is a measurement that continues to be used daily by people in the United States. It is rivaled by other measurements, however, such as degrees Celsius and degrees Kelvin. Nevertheless, Daniel Fahrenheit's contributions continue to make impacts on the world.

Daniel Fahrenheit's achievements stretch farther than just these two inventions. In addition to the mercury thermometer and the temperature scale that bears his name, Fahrenheit first demonstrated that liquids other than water have fixed boiling points that are also affected by atmospheric pressure. He is also credited with developing a method of **supercooling** water. Fahrenheit died on September 16, 1736, and was buried in The Hague, the Netherlands.

Fahrenheit restricted his original measurements to what was actually observable in the atmosphere around him.

Fahrenheit set out to measure two fixed points: the temperature of water mixed with ice and sea salt and the temperature of a healthy human body. The low point he labeled 0 degrees. The high point, the human body, he set at 96 degrees. Within this range he established water's freezing point at 32 degrees. Why these numbers? Fahrenheit originally used a twelve-point scale and established 0, 4, and 12 as these three values. Then he refined his calibrations by introducing eight smaller gradations within each larger value. Thus, his temperature for the healthy human body—96—was produced by multiplying twelve by eight. Later, when the boiling point of water was adopted as the standard high mark on the Fahrenheit scale, it was established at 212 degrees, or exactly 180 degrees above water's freezing point. This later required a retroactive adjustment of body temperature to 98.6 degrees.

The Impact of the Solution on Society

Today, Fahrenheit's influence is still felt on a daily basis. In the United States, his temperature measurement system is used; however, outside the US it is not quite as popular. Much of the rest of the world prefers to work in degrees Celsius, also developed in the eighteenth century, by Anders Celsius (1701–1744). Still, despite lacking complete global domination, Fahrenheit's inventions continue to have success more than three hundred years after their creation, making Fahrenheit a well-known name in history.

Timeline

1686
Daniel Gabriel Fahrenheit born in Danzig (modern-day Gdansk, Poland)

1701
Fahrenheit is apprenticed to a merchant to train as a bookkeeper

1714
Fahrenheit devises the first mercury thermometer

1720s
Fahrenheit begins working with different kinds of thermometers

1724
Fahrenheit publishes the only account of his methods

1736
Fahrenheit dies

Philo Farnsworth

1906–1971

Inventors in the nineteenth and twentieth centuries focused on developing many different household products—the radio, the photograph, and the vacuum cleaner. As technology developed, more devices sprang into popularity. Today, one of the most common household features is the television. It was developed in the twentieth century and plays a prominent role in modern society. People may take it for granted today, but not that long ago the television was merely a dream, something from the imagination or science fiction. There were many people who sought to make television a reality, and only a few succeeded. One of the first inventors working on the television was Philo Farnsworth, affectionately referred to as "the father of television."

81

From the Beginning

Philo Farnsworth in 1939

Philo T. Farnsworth was born into a family of Mormon farmers in a log cabin near Beaver, Utah, on August 19, 1906. During this time, electricity was just becoming widely available. Like many other young inventors, Farnsworth spent his early years tinkering with all kinds of farm machines and gadgets, many of them electrically powered.

When Farnsworth was eleven, his family relocated to Rigby, Idaho, where he developed his first invention: a thief-proof lock. He later won a prize for this device in a national inventing contest sponsored by *Science and Invention* magazine. A voracious reader of science books and magazines, Farnsworth was captivated by the work of the brilliant German-born US physicist Albert Einstein (1879–1955). By age fifteen, Farnsworth understood Einstein's photoelectric theory, which described the connection between light and electricity. Remarkably, Farnsworth could also explain Einstein's theory of relativity—one of the most complex scientific ideas ever proposed.

Defining the Problem

Farnsworth's breakthrough as an inventor came in 1922 as he guided a horse-drawn plow back and forth across his father's fields. As the machine turned up the soil into neat, parallel rows, Farnsworth realized that a picture—a pattern of light—could also be broken up into a series of parallel lines and transmitted by electricity. Greatly excited, the fifteen-year-old boy sketched the idea on a blackboard for his chemistry teacher, Justin Tolman. Although neither of them knew it at the time, this crude drawing would later play a vital part in the history of television.

After that, times grew harder for the Farnsworths. In 1922, they moved to Provo, Utah, a city south of the state capital, Salt Lake City. Farnsworth began attending Brigham Young University, but only two years into his studies, his father died and Farnsworth had to leave to support the family. During this period, he took a variety of odd jobs, from working on the railroad as an electrician to cleaning the streets, but he continued his education by taking a correspondence course from the University of Utah.

Designing the Solution

Developing a machine to turn pictures into electricity remained Farnsworth's goal. His idea was to scan a beam of light across an image in parallel rows, like a horse plowing a field. The light would be reflected back into an electronic light detector (or "image dissector," as he called it) and turned into electrical pulses that could be transmitted down a cable. At the other end, a receiving apparatus could run a similar process in reverse, using the signals to power a scanning light beam that would draw a picture on a screen faster than the eye could

Working the Television

Television is a form of communication that involves sending pictures from one place to another by electrical impulses. All objects reflect some of the light that falls onto them; that is why people can see them. In a broadcast studio, a television camera captures the light reflected off whatever is being filmed. The light is then turned into a sequence of electrical signals, using a scanning process similar to the one Philo Farnsworth originally devised.

With terrestrial television, the signals are converted into radio waves and beamed through the air using powerful antennas. Cable television sends these signals down fiber-optic cables; satellite television beams them down from orbiting spacecraft. Television sets in people's homes work in the opposite way to a television camera. First, they capture the incoming program signals from radio waves, fiber-optic cables, or satellites. Then they use the signals to build up, line by line, a pattern of light that matches exactly the pattern captured by the television camera, recreating the image captured by the camera originally.

perceive. On January 7, 1927, he patented his "image dissector," which was effectively the world's first electronic television camera.

While doing odd jobs for a charitable organization, Farnsworth met two professional fund-raisers, George Everson and Leslie Gorrell, who agreed to back his invention. The three men formed a partnership in 1926. Shortly afterward, Farnsworth married his girlfriend, Elma Gardner (nicknamed "Pem"), and they relocated to San Francisco, where the development of electronic television began in earnest. A little over a year later, on September 7, 1927, and at only twenty-one, Farnsworth made the first public demonstration of electronic television in a loft at 202 Green Street in San Francisco. In a scene reminiscent of the invention of the telephone, he stood in one room with the image dissector camera. Pem Farnsworth and George Everson were in another room with a primitive television receiver. They watched as Farnsworth transmitted the first simple picture from one room to the other.

Development of the invention continued steadily during the late 1920s, with Farnsworth attracting growing media interest. By 1928, the *San Francisco Chronicle* was publishing reports of a "young genius" who was working on a "revolutionary light machine." A few years later, *Collier's Weekly* wrote about "electrically scanned television ... destined to reach your home next year ... largely given to the world by a ... boy from Utah."

Applying the Solution

Farnsworth was not the only person trying to develop television, however. In Britain, in 1925, a Scottish engineer named John Logie Baird (1888–1946) had demonstrated an elaborate mechanical television system. Whereas Farnsworth used electronics for his image scanning, Baird opted for a clumsy, rotating wooden disc with holes cut into it that scanned an image mechanically. Farnsworth's goal was to "take all the moving parts out of television."

Lone inventors like Baird and Farnsworth were also attracting attention from large radio broadcasting companies, which began to fear that television, if successful, would harm their profits. Chief among them was the Radio Corporation of America (RCA), which dominated broadcasting in the 1920s. When its boss, David Sarnoff (1891–1971), discovered how close Farnsworth was to perfecting television, he feared the effect on RCA's business and decided to take action. He joined forces with a Russian-born television engineer, Vladimir Zworykin (1889–1982), who had been developing an alternative electronic television camera, the iconoscope, for the Westinghouse Company. In 1930, Zworykin visited Farnsworth's laboratory to see what his rival was doing; he did not tell Farnsworth that he was working for Sarnoff. Then Zworykin returned to his own laboratory and, with Sarnoff's financial backing, tried to improve on what he had seen at Farnsworth's lab.

When Zworykin was unsuccessful, Sarnoff changed his strategy. He approached Farnsworth and offered to buy him out for $100,000. Farnsworth had an idea how much his invention was worth and rejected the offer outright. Sarnoff was determined to defeat Farnsworth. He insisted that Zworykin was the rightful inventor of television because Zworykin had filed a patent for an iconoscope in 1923, four years before Farnsworth. However, because Zworykin had not demonstrated a working system, Farnsworth had gained the first patent. During the 1930s, RCA and Farnsworth fought a series of patent battles and appeals over their rival claims. Farnsworth was the ultimate victor in 1939; he was helped by the testimony of his high school teacher, Justin Tolman, who recalled the original blackboard sketch of the image dissector that his pupil had drawn for him in 1922. To Sarnoff's consternation, RCA was obliged to pay $1 million for a license to use Farnsworth's patents.

The battle with RCA had exhausted Farnsworth, leaving him depressed, in poor health, and an alcoholic. Yet that struggle was soon overshadowed by a far bigger conflict: the outbreak of World War II. As the war escalated, scientists and engineers throughout the United States became increasingly preoccupied with developing military technology, and interest in advancing television for entertainment declined. Farnsworth relocated to a farm in Brownfield, Maine, and concentrated on the Farnsworth Wood Products Company, which harvested timber for the war effort.

By the time the war ended in 1945, Farnsworth was out of touch with the electronics business and short of money. Rivals such as

RCA, who had been manufacturing military equipment, began making consumer products once more. Farnsworth was still drinking heavily and was hospitalized for depression. In 1947, most of his patents expired just as television was finally becoming popular; RCA rapidly dominated the market, much as it had done with radio years before. In 1949, David Sarnoff hosted a special twenty-fifth-anniversary program to celebrate the birth of television. Disregarding Farnsworth's work, Sarnoff introduced Vladimir Zworykin as the technology's brilliant inventor.

The Impact of the Solution on Society

The same year, now experiencing severe financial hardship, Farnsworth's company was bought out by International Telephone and Telegraph (ITT). Philo Farnsworth remained at ITT for the next eighteen years, where he was initially vice president of research and later a consultant. Although his health deteriorated, he developed a number of important military inventions, including an early warning system for missile defense and technologies that improved submarine

Television Is Born

Television was developed first in Great Britain by Scotsman John Logie Baird. Baird made the first public demonstration of a television picture in a London department store in 1925. By 1928, Baird was broadcasting television pictures across the Atlantic, from London to New York City. The following year, the British Broadcasting

John Logie Baird developed the first television in Scotland.

Inventors of Everyday Technology

detection and radar. Farnsworth also invented the first crude electron microscope and an incubator for newborn babies. Some of his inventions were more theoretical: in the late 1950s, he became one of the first people to research **nuclear fusion**, though his experiments were costly and ITT became increasingly reluctant to fund them.

In 1967, Farnsworth left ITT and moved to Brigham Young University, his old college in Utah. In recognition of his achievements, he was given an honorary doctorate of science and laboratory space, where he set up a new organization named Philo T. Farnsworth Associates (PTFA). Funding the expensive fusion research remained a problem, so members of the Farnsworth family sold all their stock, cashed in Farnsworth's life insurance policy, and borrowed from banks. It was not enough. By early 1970, the banks called in their loans and the IRS closed down the laboratory, seeking unpaid taxes. Penniless, depressed, and in poor health, Farnsworth contracted pneumonia shortly afterward and died on March 11, 1971.

By his death, Farnsworth held more than three hundred US and foreign patents, making him a truly prolific inventor. Yet his most important invention—electronic television—had failed to bring him either recognition or fortune. Although he had hoped television

Corporation (BBC) began regular television broadcasts using Baird's mechanical system.

In the United States, Baird's counterpart was inventor Charles Francis Jenkins (1867–1934), who had been trying to transmit pictures with electricity since 1894. Shortly after Baird's pioneering 1925 broadcast, Jenkins made the first public demonstration of television in the United States using a similar mechanical system. In June of that year, Jenkins was granted a US patent for his system of "Transmitting Pictures over Wireless," and he set up the first US television broadcasting station, W3XK, in 1928. Like the first home computers of the 1970s, Jenkins's early mechanical televisions were largely aimed at hobbyists, who built them from kits.

would revolutionize human education, he loathed the way it became a cheapened form of entertainment and eventually refused to let his children watch it. His wife recalled, "When Neil Armstrong landed on the moon, Phil turned to me and said, 'Pem, this has made it all worthwhile.' Before then, he wasn't too sure."

In 1987, Pem Farnsworth unveiled a bronze statue of her husband in the Utah state capitol. It bears the inscription "Father of Television." The following decade, in 1999, *Time* magazine named Farnsworth one of the one hundred most influential people of the twentieth century.

Today, televisions continue to influence the way people connect to the world around them. Much of the world today has televisions in its cities, its homes, and its public places. It is clear that in the twenty-first century Philo Farnsworth's idea has become reality. However, his involvement was largely forgotten over the years. It was only recently that he became recognized for his contributions to television technology. In 2013, he was inducted into the Academy of Television Arts & Sciences Hall of Fame, and his statue stands outside the Letterman Digital Arts Center in San Francisco.

Timeline

1906
Philo T. Farnsworth born near Beaver, Utah

1917
Farnsworth wins a prize in a national inventing contest

1922
Farnsworth gets idea that eventually leads to invention of television

1927
Farnsworth demonstrates electronic television

1939
Farnsworth wins court battles and is awarded $1 million from RCA

Late 1950s
Farnsworth is one of the first people to research nuclear fusion

1971
Farnsworth dies

Benjamin Franklin

1706–1790

As the United States began to form into the country it is today, there were several influential people whose inventions transformed society. One such person was Benjamin Franklin. He was a founding father, a diplomat, a printer and journalist, and a scientist. Today he may be known more for his presence on the fifty-dollar bill and for his political presence in the formative years of the United States of America, but Benjamin Franklin was an accomplished and creative inventor who wanted nothing more than to improve the lives of those around him.

Beginning Years

Benjamin Franklin

Benjamin Franklin, one of the most famous Americans of the eighteenth century, was born on January 17, 1706, in Boston, Massachusetts. Josiah Franklin, his father, was a soap and candle maker. What little money Josiah earned was used to support his seventeen children, of whom Benjamin was the fifteenth. Benjamin attended grammar school between the ages of eight and ten, then left to work in his father's shop, where he helped by cutting candlewicks, molding wax, and running errands. Around this time, he also developed a passion for swimming and created his first invention: a set of swim fins that could propel him quickly through the water.

At age twelve, he became an apprentice to his brother James, a printer in Boston. From James, Franklin learned the printing trade that would soon make him famous. During the day he helped James print his newspaper, the *New England Courant*; in the evening he studied English. He would read essays from great books and then try to rewrite them in his own words. Gradually, he mastered an impressive style. One day, for a joke, Franklin started writing funny letters to his brother's paper and submitting them under the pseudonym Mrs. Silence Dogood. Although the letters were popular with readers, James was furious when he found out who had written them. The brothers had a falling out, and Benjamin decided to leave Boston.

Defining the Problem

After a brief period in New York City, the seventeen-year-old Benjamin Franklin traveled to Philadelphia. He found work as a printer and made friends with William Keith, the governor of Pennsylvania. Keith advised Franklin to go to London to finish training as a printer, even offering to pay his expenses. Franklin accepted the offer, but Keith's money was never forthcoming.

When he arrived in London, he was stranded and had to use his printing skills to find work to support himself. After spending about eighteen months in London, where he met many famous writers and publishers, he had saved enough money to return to Philadelphia. There, in 1728, he started his own print shop—he was only twenty-two.

Franklin worked hard at his printing business, becoming wealthy and successful. He was the official printer for Philadelphia, New Jersey, Delaware, and Maryland, but he became better known for an amusing book, *Poor Richard's Almanac*, printed annually from 1732 to 1757. This almanac combined a calendar and weather forecasts with amusing stories and sayings. Many of the proverbs of this book are still popular, including, "Haste makes waste" and, "Early to bed, early to rise, makes a man healthy, wealthy, and wise."

Some of Franklin's best-known inventions date from this time. In 1740, he began to think about the way people heated their homes by burning fuel in large open fireplaces. After some experimenting, he invented what became known as the Franklin stove: a sturdy cast-iron basket with a large, open front that drew in more air, burned less fuel more efficiently, and gave off less smoke and more heat than an open-hearth fireplace. Often made in a freestanding form, it could be placed in the middle of a room to warm the area more evenly. Franklin's stove was also safer because the metal basket held the burning fuel more securely.

Designing the Solution

Most of Franklin's inventions were designed to overcome everyday nuisances. Some, such as his invention of bifocal eyeglasses, were inspired by his own experiences. Oftentimes, when people pass the age of forty, their eyesight changes in a way that makes seeing close objects difficult. As Franklin already wore eyeglasses, he was confronted with the inconvenience of needing two different pairs, one for seeing close up and another for looking into the distance. This inspired Franklin to invent bifocals: he took his two pairs of eyeglasses, cut the lenses in half, and then joined the opposite halves together to create a single pair for seeing close up when he looked down or into the distance when he looked up.

Applying the Solution

Franklin had many good ideas, but not all of them were for inventions—some were ideas for improving society. From the 1730s on, he devoted much of his time to the public services of Philadelphia. He had the idea to pay for a "city watch," as it was then known, which became the city's first police force. He campaigned successfully for improvements to street cleaning, paving, and lighting. He helped found a hospital. He also organized the first volunteer fire company in America. His love of knowledge and books prompted him to establish what is widely believed to have been the country's first public library; it housed books, a museum of scientific instruments, and a collection of mounted and stuffed wildlife specimens, including a pelican. Later, Franklin founded an academy, opened in 1751, which eventually became the University of Pennsylvania.

Many of his civic improvements were concerned with the post office. Between 1737 and 1753, Franklin served as deputy postmaster to Philadelphia. He quickly identified many problems with the postal service and put improvements in place. Postal fees were charged according to the weight of each item and how far it had to be carried from the sender to the receiver. However, no one knew the distances between cities at that time, so disputes often arose about how much to charge. Franklin solved this problem with another of his inventions, the odometer. This was a simple measuring device attached to the wheels of a mail carriage. As the carriage rolled along, the odometer's dials spun, recording the exact distance traveled. With that information, a precise mailing fee could be calculated.

By the end of the 1740s, Franklin had earned enough from his printing business to retire. He bought a large 300-acre (121-hectare) farm near Burlington, New Jersey, and began to devote himself to the study of electricity. Almost nothing was then known about the subject: what electricity was, how it flowed, and how it could be stored were all questions waiting to be answered. Franklin played a major part in unraveling the mystery. Electrical research earned him world fame in the 1750s, when he published his results in a series of pamphlets (later collected into a book, *Experiments and Observations on Electricity*). Soon translated into French, Italian, and German, the pamphlets helped European scientists begin to regard electricity as a usable form of energy rather than a curiosity of the natural world. Franklin's work was an immense breakthrough (although its fundamental importance was not immediately realized) and did have an immediate practical benefit—it led to one of his most famous inventions: the lightning rod.

In 1752, in one of the most famous scientific experiments in history, Franklin went out in a thunderstorm to fly his kite. After several years studying electricity, he had arrived at the theory that lightning and electricity were somehow connected; all he had to do was prove it. With his kite dipping and rattling high in the air, he tied a metal key to the end of the kite's long, wet string. When he moved one of his knuckles toward the key, he felt a small tingle: electricity was traveling down the string from the storm, through his finger, and running through his body to the ground. Franklin was lucky not to have been killed.

The experiment demonstrated that a lightning bolt is a massive discharge of electricity from the sky to the ground. Such an immense

Franklin's Many Inventions

Lightning rods, busybodies, stoves, eyeglasses, and swim fins—these are just some of the devices Benjamin Franklin brought into being during his long and highly productive career as an inventor. Unlike many inventors before and since, Franklin was not motivated by money. His printing business had made him wealthy, so he did not need his inventions to support him or add to his wealth. Some of his inventions would have earned him a fortune, yet he steadfastly refused to patent any of them.

When he developed the Franklin stove, the governor of Pennsylvania offered him a patent on the invention so he could make money from it, but he refused. He wanted the stove to be manufactured inexpensively to make it affordable to as many people as possible. Commenting on this in his autobiography, he said, "As we enjoy great advantages from the inventions of others, we should be glad of an opportunity to serve others by any invention of ours; and this we should do freely and generously."

amount of electrical energy can kill people instantly, set buildings on fire, and make trees explode by boiling the liquids inside them dry. However, Franklin saw that lightning could be tamed by creating a more direct path for the electricity to follow. He invented the lightning rod: a strip of metal that runs down the side of a high building, carrying the electricity in lightning safely to ground.

The kite experiment confirmed Franklin's theory that electricity was a kind of fluid that could flow from place to place. Charles Du Fay (1698–1739), a French scientist, had explored this idea twenty years earlier and was convinced that electricity was of two kinds. However, through his experiments, Franklin came to a very different conclusion: electricity was of a single kind but could flow in different directions. If it flowed into an object, that object would effectively gain electricity: Franklin described this as a negative charge. If it flowed out of an object, that object would lose electricity, gaining a positive charge. The movement of positive and negative charges around a circuit eventually came to be known as electric current.

Increasing the understanding of electricity was one of Franklin's most famous contributions to science. Later, he carried out important experiments on the way heat flows. He was one of the first to understand how evaporation can cool liquids and solids. While wearing a wet shirt on a hot day, he noticed that he stayed cool because water evaporating from the shirt removed heat from his body. Thus, he concluded: "One may see the possibility of freezing a man to death even on a warm summer's day."

In the 1740s, Franklin observed that stormy weather does not always travel in the same direction as the wind. This observation helped to improve the accuracy of weather forecasts. Around thirty years later, Franklin investigated another important influence on the weather: the **Gulf Stream**. Although Franklin did not discover the Gulf Stream (sailors had known of it since the 1500s), he measured its temperature, speed, and depth and also drew the earliest maps of it.

The Impact of the Solution on Society

Franklin had already achieved much as a printer, public servant, scientist, and inventor. In the 1750s, a new phase of his life began that would make him a world-famous statesman. In 1754, conflict between France and Britain spread to their colonies in North America, in what is referred to as the French and Indian War. French soldiers in Canada joined forces with Native Americans and began raiding Pennsylvania, then still a British colony. In 1767, Franklin was dispatched to London to raise support for the people of Pennsylvania from the king of

How Electricity Works

Franklin's experiments in electricity were groundbreaking because they demonstrated that electricity could be made to move from one place to another in a controlled way. This realization marked the birth of electric current. Unlike previous theories of electricity, which were only partly correct, the theory of positive and negative charges was a more complete explanation of what electricity was actually doing. Thus, Franklin's biggest contribution was to put the science of electricity on the correct conceptual path, which helped humans swiftly move forward in their understanding and use of this elemental force.

Two Italian scientists, Luigi Galvani (1737–1798) and Alessandro Volta (1745–1827), read Franklin's writings on electricity. In 1800, Volta ushered in the modern age of electricity when he became the first person to make a practical electric battery. Other pioneers, including the English scientist Michael Faraday (1791–1867) and the prolific US inventor Thomas Edison (1847–1931), then turned electricity into a useful everyday source of power. Franklin's original work was crucial to these advances.

In 1898, just over a century after Franklin's death, his research helped scientists discover the electron, the tiny particle inside atoms that carries electricity around circuits. In fact, the concept of positive and negative charge, which Franklin delineated, is central to the modern scientific understanding of atoms. Robert Millikan (1868–1953), an American physicist who won a Nobel Prize for his pioneering work with electrons, described Franklin's kite experiment as "probably the most fundamental thing ever done in the field of electricity."

This painting depicts Benjamin Franklin returning to Philadelphia after his trip to London in 1775.

England. He remained there for eight years, during which time he met and shared his ideas with some of the most famous scientists in Europe.

When he returned to Philadelphia in 1775, the opening battles of the War of Independence had already been fought. Franklin was now sixty-nine and was widely respected for his wisdom. He was one of the five men who drafted and signed the Declaration of Independence in 1776. As the war progressed, Franklin spent time in France, seeking backing for America in the fight against Britain.

When Benjamin Franklin returned again to Philadelphia, on September 14, 1785, practically the entire city turned out to welcome him home. Cannons were fired, bells were rung, and the celebration lasted a week. Although he was nearly eighty and somewhat frail, he remained an active statesman. For the next three years, he served as president of the Pennsylvania Executive Council. He also helped to draw up and sign the Constitution of the United States in 1787. One of his last acts was to sign a petition to the US Congress on February 12, 1790, recommending the abolition of slavery.

In poor health, Franklin spent his last years at home, where he devised ingenious inventions to make life easier. He constructed a rocking chair with curved rollers attached to the legs so he could move back and forth. His writing chair had a large piece of wood attached to one arm so he did not have to sit at a desk to work. Unable to reach books on high shelves, he invented a mechanical arm to help him lift them down. For the last year of his life, Franklin was bedridden and in constant pain. He devised a pulley system to lock and unlock his door while he was lying in his bed. Reputedly, he also invented the famous "busybody," three carefully positioned mirrors that allowed him to see visitors at his front door without getting up. Franklin died on April 17, 1790, at age eighty-four.

Benjamin Franklin influenced society in ways never before experienced. Many of his inventions would revolutionize the world, and his legacy lives on even today. Through his experiments and knowledge, Franklin became an icon. He was determined to share his ideas with everyone and not accept payment for the use of his creations. Today, Franklin's is still a well-known name, and his mark on history will continue to be remembered and celebrated.

Timeline

1706
Benjamin Franklin born in Boston, Massachusetts

1718
Franklin becomes a printer's apprentice in Boston

1728
Franklin starts his own printing business in Philadelphia

1732
Franklin begins publishing *Poor Richard's Almanac*

1740
Franklin invents the Franklin stove

Late 1740s
Franklin retires from his printing business and studies electricity

1752
Franklin conducts his kite experiment

1776
Franklin helps write the Declaration of Independence

1790
Franklin dies

King C. Gillette

1855–1932

For many centuries, men have relied on sharp blades to shave their faces. Today, there is more than one shaving option: electric razors, disposable razors, or old-fashioned straight razors and shaving brushes. However, this was not always the case. Prior to the early twentieth century, many men shaved with safety razors that required sharpening on a leather strap. Without frequent sharpening, the razor would become dull. A solution to these types of razors came about in 1901, when a man named King C. Gillette developed a disposable safety razor that changed the way men shaved.

Starting Out

King Camp Gillette was born in Fond du Lac, Wisconsin, in 1855 but moved to Chicago with his family at the age of four. His parents could both be considered inventors of a sort. King's father developed new devices and tinkered with technology as a hobby, and his mother created new recipes in the kitchen. In 1887, she published many of her "inventions" in *The Whitehouse Cookbook*, which remained in print for more than a century.

King Camp Gillette
ca. 1906

In 1871, the family lost everything in the great Chicago fire and relocated to New York City. Gillette's father found work as a patent agent and regaled the family with stories of the new inventions that came across his desk. Gillette left school at age seventeen to begin a career as a traveling salesman. He also had "a tinkerer's bent," as one journalist put it. By 1890, Gillette had secured patents for a few inventions, but he never had success developing a business with any of them.

Defining the Problem

At the age of thirty-six, Gillette became a New York and New England sales representative for the Baltimore Seal Company, which manufactured seals for pumping equipment and beverage containers. The president of the company, William Painter, built his fortune on one invention in particular, the Crown Cork, a cork-lined bottle cap.

Painter had a profound effect on Gillette's life. He urged Gillette to find his own "Crown Cork"—that is, something that was used once and then thrown away so that the customer would keep coming back for more. In essence, Painter was pushing Gillette to invent something disposable. Despite some initial skepticism, Gillette took Painter's words to heart, and for years he tried to find the perfect idea.

Designing the Solution

In the spring of 1895, Gillette finally found his version of the Crown Cork. As is the case with many other great inventions, the idea came to Gillette at an unexpected moment: he thought of it in the bathroom.

One morning, Gillette woke and tried to shave, but his Star Safety Razor had become very, very dull.

Gillette began to imagine a new kind of razor, one that did not need continual sharpening. He later wrote that he wanted something "made cheap enough to do away with honing and stropping and permit the user to replace dull blades by new ones." Gillette envisioned a small, square sheet of steel, fashioned into a thin, double-sided blade. It would be safe, easy to use, cheap, and, on the advice of Painter, disposable.

Gillette's invention, although simple in theory, proved so complex in reality that six years were needed to develop a workable prototype. Gillette was living in Boston when the idea struck him, so he visited the nearby Massachusetts Institute of Technology (MIT) to discuss his plan with some engineers who worked with steel. Each told him it would be impossible to create a blade as small, hard, thin, and inexpensive as he wanted.

Finally, in 1900, Gillette met engineer and inventor William Nickerson, who had been educated at MIT and who had established a reputation as a skilled inventor. Although Nickerson, like the other scientists, was somewhat skeptical at first, he took on the challenge to make Gillette's blade. They founded the American Safety Razor Company in 1901.

The two men worked in a one-room workshop above a fish market on Boston's waterfront. Gillette and some early investors put about $5,000 into research and development. Nickerson designed a machine that could make inexpensive 40-gauge blades that were 0.88 inch (2.2 centimeters) wide and just 0.006 inch (0.015 cm) thick. With those specifications, one pound of steel could create almost four hundred blades.

Gillette took Nickerson's blades and developed a blade carrier attached to a handle. It was a success. Although Nickerson developed the blade, his name was too close to the word "nick" so often associated with shaving. So, the Gillette Safety Razor was born. In 1902, Gillette and Nickerson renamed their venture the Gillette Safety Razor Company.

The first safety razor from Gillette in 1901

Applying the Solution

Production of Gillette razors did not begin until 1903. The company
struggled under the weight of more than $12,000 in debt. One
acquaintance of the two men told a reporter for the *Wall Street
Journal*, "Delays were so serious that Gillette was almost persuaded
to shut down and say good-bye to all the rainbows." The sales for that
year were meager: 51 razors and 168 blades.

The next year saw a quick reversal. On November 15, 1904, Gillette was granted US Patent No. 775,134, for "certain new and useful improvements in razors." Gillette saturated the market with his product, often selling the razors at a discount or giving them away free. The company sold more than 90,000 razors and 124,000 blades that year. Gillette put his portrait and signature on every package. The product's success ensured that he quickly became one of the most familiar faces of his day. Some have argued that Gillette blades were as recognizable a product as Coca-Cola or Ford automobiles.

In 1905, Gillette expanded abroad, opening a sales office in London. By 1908, the company had production facilities in Canada, England, France, and Germany, in addition to those in the United States. By 1910, Gillette razors dominated the market and Gillette was a millionaire. At a decade old in 1911, the company was selling thirty-five million blades per year. By 1915, it was selling more than seventy million blades worldwide.

Gillette and Utopia

Gillette's incredible success as a businessman is somewhat ironic given his other lifelong passion—the establishment of a socialist utopia. In 1894, before the development of the disposable blade, Gillette wrote a book called *The Human Drift*. An anticapitalist book in which he criticized the business world and called competition the root of all evil, *The Human Drift* advocated that all industry be taken over by one, supposedly benevolent, corporation. As an antidote to the grimy cities that were born of the Industrial Revolution, Gillette proposed a new kind of world order, a pollution-free, efficient, hive-like commune powered by hydro-energy created by Niagara Falls.

Gillette wrote *World Corporation* in 1910, building on his original ideas. Before World War I, Gillette asked Theodore Roosevelt to serve as leader of a utopian society he hoped to build in what was then the Arizona Territory. Roosevelt declined, as did Henry Ford. Gillette wrote a final book, *The People's Corporation*, in 1924.

A Business Mindset

The business model that Gillette developed is nearly as famous as the razor itself. Gillette sold many of the razors at a loss and even gave them away—not just at the beginning of the business but throughout. He realized that giving razors away for nothing or next to nothing would build his market base. With a large base of men using his razor, in the long run, he could more than make up "lost" sales revenue through blade sales. Men might buy one razor in a lifetime, but they would buy dozens of blades each year. The razor is an example of what is now called a loss leader.

Gillette employed this business model again when the United States entered World War I. He developed razor sets for the US Army, which he sold to the government at reduced rates. In return, more than 3.5 million soldiers used his razors and blades and many of them became customers for life.

Advertising also played a big role in the success of the Gillette razor. In a memo from 1912, Gillette told his executives that "the whole success" of the company rode on ads. The company was one of the first to use sports figures to promote razors. Today, sports figures and other celebrities sell not just razors but a wide range of consumer products, such as shoes, clothing, cars, and kitchen appliances.

The Impact of the Solution on Society

With the success of the Gillette razor came imitation, and for many years Gillette was embroiled in patent battles. In later life, he was more a figurehead for the company than its leader. Eventually, he turned his interests to a new project, an unsuccessful attempt to extract oil from shale.

Gillette, who had resigned as president of the company in 1931, died in 1932 in Southern California, where he had bought land to grow oranges and dates. He was nearly bankrupt as a result of the Great Depression.

The Gillette Safety Razor Company went on to become remarkably successful. The first electric shaver, the Gillette dry shaver, was introduced in 1938. In time, the company's product line included Foamy shaving cream, Right Guard antiperspirant,

Oral-B dental products, and other, nonpersonal goods, such as pens. At the turn of the twenty-first century, the company had annual sales of more than $9.9 billion. Gillette was acquired by Procter & Gamble in 2005.

Gillette's innovation led to improving an already existing device and making it more functional for a modern audience. His influence on the shaving industry continues to this day, as Gillette is one of the leading companies in safety razor production. King Gillette's legacy lives on in the company and products that bear his name.

Timeline

1855
King Camp Gillette born in Fond du Lac, Wisconsin

1872
Gillette drops out of school to become a traveling salesman

1895
Gillette gets idea for a disposable razor

1901
Gillette and William Nickerson found the American Safety Razor Company

1903
Production of Gillette razors begins

1931
Gillette resigns as president of company

1932
Gillette dies

Beulah Henry

1887–1973

During the early decades of the 1900s, few women inventors embarked on the journey to becoming noteworthy inventors. This was not for lack of interest but rather due to difficulties during a time period when mainly men were granted recognition for their accomplishments. Within the small group of women who did take up the task, one woman is known today as an accomplished inventor and holder of forty-nine patents for different creations. Beulah Henry continues to prevail in the history of women inventors and inventions, inspiring others to pursue their dreams.

Early Days

Although Henry was a prolific inventor, not much is known about her life. Born in Memphis, Tennessee, in 1887, Beulah Louise Henry is believed to be a descendent of Patrick Henry, the American revolutionary who cried, "Give me liberty or give me death!"

Some sources suggest that Henry's knack for invention began early on, when she was a young girl who sketched her creations. Art was a family interest; her father was an authority on art, her mother was an artist, and her brother was a songwriter. Records show that she attended Presbyterian and Elizabeth colleges in Charlotte, North Carolina, graduating in 1909.

Defining the Problem

In 1912 at age twenty-five, while still living in North Carolina, Henry received her first patent, for an ice cream freezer with a vacuum seal. The following year, she patented a handbag and parasol. Her early success prompted her to move to New York City.

In New York, Henry created one of her best-known inventions, an umbrella with a detachable snap-on cloth cover that permitted women

Lady Edison

A young Thomas Edison in 1878

Henry is remembered as "Lady Edison," a nickname bestowed upon her by the US Patent Office. Some, in particular the women engineers who have helped keep Beulah Henry in the history books, find the appellation condescending because Henry was clearly an outstanding inventor in her own right. Still, the number of patented inventions compared to her contemporary, Edison, earned her the nickname. For her work she continues to be admired as a talented inventor.

to coordinate their rain gear with different outfits. When Henry first suggested the idea, umbrella manufacturers of the day told her it could not be done. She forged ahead despite their skepticism and created the product in 1924. Her umbrellas would earn her $50,000—a considerable sum in the 1920s—and a prominent spot in the windows of Lord and Taylor, one of New York City's leading department stores. On the basis of the umbrella's success, she founded the Henry Umbrella and Parasol Company.

During the 1920s, Henry also invented various products related to sponges, including the Latho, which was a sponge with a special compartment that opened and snapped shut to hold a bar of soap inside. The product also floated, to help bathers locate the soap in the bath. Manufacturers proved unable to cut sponges to produce the Latho correctly, so Henry developed a machine that could. In 1929, she patented "Dolly Dips," the children's version of the Latho.

By age forty, Henry had founded her second company, the B. L. Henry Company of New York, which produced a variety of her inventions. She was one of the few of that era to have inventions patented in four different countries and to have two businesses in her name.

Designing the Solution

Another domain of Henry's inventing was toys, including several types of dolls. The most famous, perhaps, was the Miss Illusion doll, from 1935. Miss Illusion had interchangeable wigs—one blonde, one brunette—and a reversible dress. The doll's eyes, which opened and closed by a mechanism inside the head, were also changeable, from blue to brown. Henry invented dolls with spring-loaded limbs and bendable arms, dolls that could kick, blink, eat, and even talk. Another doll had a radio inside.

Henry also produced educational products for children, including Kiddie Klock, which taught children to tell time; and Cross Country, a board game that taught children about US geography. Unlike her other inventions, many of these toys were never patented and were simply sold to various toy companies.

Beulah Louise Henry models one of her toy dolls.

Applying the Solution

During the 1930s and 1940s, Henry shifted her focus to machines—most notably, the typewriter. Invented in 1867 by Christopher Latham Sholes (1819–1890), the typewriter revolutionized communication and became one of the most common implements in everyday business. Between 1932 and 1964, Henry received eleven patents related to the typewriter. Her first was for the "protograph," a machine that worked with a manual typewriter to create several copies of a single document without using carbon paper. During World War II, with carbon shortages, the protograph proved very useful. Other inventions included devices for feeding documents into and aligning documents for typewriters and duplicating machines. In 1937, she invented a cash register that could write like a typewriter for the National Cash Register Company.

In 1939, Henry was hired as an inventor by Nicholas Machine Works. The company provided her with a lab and technical staff. While there, she was credited with several dozen inventions, some of which—as had happened with the Latho—required her to develop not only the product but also the means of production.

The Impact of the Solution on Society

During her amazing career, Henry apparently never married. She spent much of her life living in hotels, in particular New York's Hotel Victoria. Records show she was a member of many city establishments, including the Museum of Natural History, the Audubon Society, and the League for Animals. Various mentions in the press suggest that Henry enjoyed a somewhat public, if enigmatic, persona. Indeed, news stories mentioned her "superb auburn hair" and her "commanding presence." She told reporters of her fondness for painting. She continued to invent well into old age, receiving her final patent in 1970, at the age of eighty-three. She died three years later.

What is most significant about Henry's career, aside from the sheer number of her inventions, was that, unlike most women of her day, she profited significantly from her work. Many inventions by women in that era were credited to their husbands—at that time, inventions by women accounted for less than 1 percent of all US patents.

While not all of her products made it into the present day, Beulah Henry is remembered for her many achievements and, above all, her determination to keep inventing. She was part of a minority group of inventors at that time, and her contributions were immense and important to inspiring other women inventors to aspire for similar success.

Timeline

1887
Beulah Louise Henry is born in Memphis, Tennessee

1912
Henry receives her first patent

1924
Henry creates a new type of umbrella

1927
Henry founds the B. L. Henry Company of New York

1932–1964
Henry receives eleven patents for inventions related to the typewriter

1939
Henry is hired as an inventor by the Nicholas Machine Works

1970
Henry receives her final patents

1973
Henry dies

Walter Hunt

1796–1859

Sometimes inventors and their inventions become lost in the folds of history. People cannot call them to mind upon hearing their name or creation, and it may take some searching before information on them is unearthed. One such person is Walter Hunt. Few today know that he was one of the most accomplished inventors of the nineteenth century or that he invented an early kind of sewing machine nearly twenty years before Elias Howe (1819–1867) received credit. Still fewer know that his most famous and lasting product exists today: the modern safety pin. Hunt was a man known in his era, but his achievements have become buried over time, as more and more inventors with more creations come into the forefront of history.

An Inventor Begins

Walter Hunt

As with many other mostly forgotten inventors, very little is known about Hunt's life. He was born near Martinsburg, New York, and lived most of his life in New York City. When and whom he married are unclear, but he certainly had a family. In 1935, Clinton N. Hunt, a great-grandson, self-published a pamphlet that included descriptions of more than two dozen of Hunt's inventions. Hunt was by trade a mechanic. Most accounts suggest that, despite his wealth of inventions, he never became wealthy himself.

Defining the Problem

In his early life, Hunt worked as a farmer in Lowville, New York. One of his tasks was to design machinery for local mills. This inspired him to design other objects. In 1826, he moved to New York City and received his first patent. He continued to enjoy designing things. Other inventions included a rifle, ice plows, and a knife sharpener. It wasn't long before Hunt wanted to create more.

Designing the Solution

Hunt invented the first lockstitch sewing machine around 1834. It was not the first sewing machine, but it was the first machine to utilize lockstitches, in which two threads interlock at a seam, instead of trying to mimic hand-sewn stitches. Hunt's machine was also the first to utilize a curved, eye-pointed needle—another invention by Hunt.

Hunt never patented his sewing machine. He allegedly lost interest when he thought the machine would cause unemployment by putting seamstresses and tailors out of work. (Such an outcome was unlikely, as his sewing machine could produce only straight seams, and only for a few inches at a time.) In 1846, Elias Howe patented a similar lockstitch sewing machine. A few years later, Isaac Singer infringed on Howe's copyright. In the legal battle that ensued between Singer and Howe, the court decreed that Hunt had invented the eye-pointed needle, but nothing more. Singer was left to reap the rewards and riches of the sewing machine, which has often been called one of the most important inventions in history.

Applying the Solution

The sewing machine was not the only time Hunt let a potential fortune slip through his fingers. Fifteen years later, he invented and patented the safety pin but then sold his rights to it for next to nothing.

Of the stories that still circulate about Hunt, the most famous is that of the safety pin. Hunt needed to pay off a $15 debt. While he pondered his options, he twisted an 8-inch (20 cm) length of brass wire. After three hours, he stared at the bent piece of metal and realized he had created something useful—a new type of pin.

Hunt had coiled the wire so that it had a spring in the middle. He created a "safety" clasp at one end of the wire. This design, which by now is familiar to almost everyone, allowed the remaining sharp end of the wire to be forced by the spring into the clasp. The tension between the spring and the clasp made the pin strong, and the clasp itself kept whoever was wearing the pin from being pricked. In the patent application Hunt wrote of "the perfect convenience of inserting these into the dress, without danger of bending the pin, or wounding the fingers."

Hunt's safety pin was obviously not the first device to be invented to hold clothes together. Pins had been used since ancient times. The Greeks and Romans used a type of pin, known as a fibula, to fasten their robes. Hunt's pin was also not the first safety pin. In 1842, Thomas Woodward, another New Yorker, patented a straight pin with a safety shield, which he called a "Victorian shielded shawl and diaper pin." Hunt's improvement lay in the coiled spring.

Hunt received US Patent No. 6,281 for what he called a "dress pin" on April 10, 1849. He quickly sold his patent for $400, according to most sources, to pay a debt. One can only wonder if he ever suspected that the safety pin, as it came to be called, might have earned him a fortune.

The Impact of the Solution on Society

Hunt invented many other devices, obtaining twenty-six patents by the time of his death in 1859. Inventions attributed to Hunt include a streetcar bell, a fountain pen, a tree saw, an ice plow for ships, a shoe heel, road sweeping machinery, machines for making nails and rivets, a revolver, and a type of bullet. A knife sharpener Hunt patented in 1829 is still used.

In his lifetime, Hunt earned mentions in various magazines, including *Atlantic Monthly* and *Scientific American*, but he did not create a lasting reputation for himself. Whereas some inventors used marketing savvy to ensure their success, Hunt invented, it seems, for invention's sake.

Today the safety pin continues to aid people around the world in holding clothes and other materials together. Its design has changed little over the years, and there are now many different sizes of safety pin. It appears Hunt's invention will remain as one of the most practical inventions of the nineteenth century.

Timeline

1796
Walter Hunt born near Martinsburg, New York

1829
Hunt patents a knife sharpener

ca. 1834
Hunt invents the lockstitch sewing machine

1846
A similar sewing machine is patented by Elias Howe

1849
Hunt patents the safety pin

1859
Hunt dies

Lonnie Johnson

1949–

For many children growing up in the late twentieth and early twenty-first centuries, there came a time during the hot months of summer when children wanted to cool down. A popular game to play involved water guns. One of the leading types of squirt gun was the Super Soaker, a large toy that would make cooling down easy. The inventor of this toy was a man who refused to specialize in one particular area of invention. Lonnie Johnson has contributed many ideas and products to the world, but his most famous is the Super Soaker, which Johnson invented while he worked for NASA's Jet Propulsion Laboratory in 1982. It was a toy that continues its popularity today.

Lonnie Johnson holds his Super Soaker patent in 1992.

Inventing the Inventor

Lonnie Johnson was born in 1949, the third of six children. He grew up in Mobile, Alabama, where his father worked as a truck driver for the US Air Force, and where his mother worked as a nurse's aide. Early in life, Johnson showed an interest in machinery, frequently taking his siblings' toys apart to see how they worked.

Johnson also became interested in rocketry at a young age. This interest led to some dramatic incidents. One time he was mixing rocket fuel in the kitchen when the fuel started a fire, which was put out without any serious injury. When Johnson was fourteen, he took some of his rocket fuel to school. A classmate set the fuel on fire in a hallway, and Johnson was taken to the police station and accused of trying to blow up the school.

Still, Johnson did well in high school. In 1968, he built a remote-controlled robot that won a national engineering competition. He won a scholarship to Tuskegee University, where he earned a bachelor's of science in 1972 and a master's degree in nuclear engineering in 1974.

Defining the Problem

A few months after receiving his master's degree, Johnson joined the air force. While in the service, he worked in engineering positions in a variety of fields, ranging from nuclear power to computing. In the early 1980s he was transferred to the Jet Propulsion Laboratory (JPL) in Pasadena, California, where he worked on developing satellites and probes for various space missions, including the *Galileo* probe of Jupiter and the *Mars Observer* project.

Johnson enjoyed his work, but he became frustrated with the **bureaucracy** and restrictions of the air force and JPL. He tinkered at home, working on various inventions of his own.

Designing the Solution

One day in 1982, Johnson was in his bathroom working on a new kind of water pump. He attached a high-pressure nozzle to the sink and was surprised when the water shot all the way across the bathroom.

Johnson thought the nozzle might be used to make a water gun for his nine-year-old daughter, so he created a prototype for her. The powerful water gun proved a huge hit in the neighborhood, and Johnson realized that he might have a marketable product.

Applying the Solution

Johnson filed for a patent for the new water gun the next year. It would take many more years for the Super Soaker to become a reality, however. Johnson was not a manufacturer, and he did not have the money to build and market the gun himself. He spent the next several years trying to interest toy companies and investment banks in the water gun and his many other inventions.

"There is no short easy route to success ... It takes a lot of hard work and a bit of luck to be successful."
—Lonnie Johnson

In 1987, an investment firm agreed to finance and develop some of his ideas. Johnson, assuming that the deal would go through and that he would have a new career, quit the air force and JPL and arranged to sell his home. At the last minute, however, the firm **reneged** on the agreement. Johnson was able to get his job with JPL back, but when he backed out of his agreement to sell his house, he was sued.

Johnson continued his efforts to sell his water gun. Finally, during a trade show in New York City, an executive from a small toy company called Larami Corporation saw the gun and liked it. Larami reached a licensing agreement with Johnson in 1989, and his gun, first called the Power Drencher and then the Super Soaker, went on the market at last.

The Super Soaker was far more powerful than the standard water gun. An ordinary water gun had a range of just a few feet, but a Super

Soaker could hit a target 40 feet (12 m) away. Sales for the gun took off in 1991 after Johnny Carson, host of *The Tonight Show*, used a Super Soaker to blast his staff during the program.

The Impact of the Solution on Society

By 1992, sales of Super Soakers topped $200 million. The success of the gun gave rise to a slew of improvements and modifications, resulting in an entire line of Super Soaker water guns, as well as an untold number of imitations. Three years later, Larami sold the Super Soaker line to Hasbro, Inc., the second-largest toy maker in the United States.

How Water Guns Work

Before the advent of the Super Soaker, water guns had a simple design. Water was held in a reservoir chamber, usually located in the handle of the gun. A second chamber was connected to the first through a one-way valve, which was connected to the nozzle.

The gun's trigger acted as a pump. When the trigger was released, it would suck water from the reservoir into the second chamber, and the one-way valve would hold the water there. When the trigger was squeezed, the water would be expelled from the second chamber out the nozzle of the gun. As the squeezing of the trigger was the only force that expelled the water out of the gun, the gun did not shoot much water and did not shoot it very far.

The Super Soaker, in contrast, eliminated the pumping action of the conventional water-gun trigger. Instead, the gun had two reservoir chambers, one of which was airtight. Before shooting the gun, the user would pump water from one reservoir chamber into the second, airtight one, to ready the gun to fire. As a result of this pumping action, the air within the second chamber would become compressed. Instead of acting as a pump, the trigger opened a connection between the second chamber and the nozzle. Once that connection was open, the compressed air forced the water out of the gun at high pressure.

Super Soakers are still popular with kids today.

The success of the Super Soaker allowed Johnson to resign from the JPL and to become a full-time inventor. He currently runs Johnson Research & Development in Atlanta, Georgia, a firm that has developed toys such as Nerf guns and air-powered rockets. In addition to toys, Johnson has received research contracts from various US government agencies to develop devices ranging from rechargeable batteries made of thin film to environmentally safe refrigeration systems and advanced fuel cells.

Today the Super Soaker continues to have success. It is considered one of the most popular toys in recent decades and has gone through many transformations, with new and improved Super Soaker products. Lonnie Johnson likewise had had success with other inventions. In 2008, he won the Popular Mechanics Breakthrough Award for his thermo-electrochemical converter. He also has over eighty patented products. It is clear that Johnson has had a great influence on toy making and the world of invention.

Timeline

1949
Lonnie Johnson born; he grows up in Mobile, Alabama

1968
Johnson wins a national engineering competition

1974
Johnson earns a master's degree in nuclear engineering

1982
Johnson creates a high-velocity squirt gun

1989
The Super Soaker goes on the market

1995
The Super Soaker line of products is sold to Hasbro, Inc.

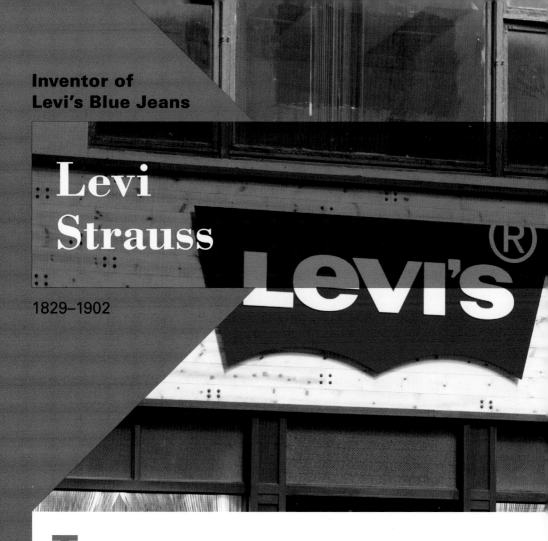

Levi Strauss

1829–1902

Today it may seem normal to pull on a pair of jeans when getting ready for school, to visit friends, or sometimes even to go to work. However, that was not always the case. Before the arrival of Levi Strauss, jeans as we know them did not exist. Men and sometimes women wore pants made from different materials. Over the years, blue jeans have evolved. They have been symbols of the American West, of rebellion, and today of the modern person. It is a type of clothing that has influenced people and has become standard in everyday fashion.

Becoming an Inventor

Levi Strauss ca. 1850

Levi Strauss was born Loeb Strauss in 1829, in what is now Buttenheim, Germany. His family was Jewish. After his father, Hirsch, died of tuberculosis, and because of the growing poverty and anti-Semitism in Bavaria at the time, he moved to the United States with his mother and two sisters in 1847. They joined two half brothers, who had already moved to the Lower East Side of New York City to set up a dry goods business. J. Strauss Brothers and Co. sold, among other items, canvas, cloth, linen, and clothing. Strauss's father had sold cloth and other dry goods door-to-door in Buttenheim.

After three years in America working for his brothers' stores, Loeb changed his name to Levi. In January 1853, he became an American citizen and headed west to San Francisco to establish the West Coast outpost of the family business.

San Francisco was still caught up in the economic boom ushered in by the gold rush of the late 1840s. Strauss, just twenty-four years old, arrived in March 1853 and set up a wholesale dry goods business, Levi Strauss and Co., near the city's waterfront.

Defining the Problem

Strauss developed a reputation as an honest and fair merchant, and Levi Strauss and Co. grew rapidly into a successful business. Soon, Levi Strauss and Co. was selling cloth, blankets, handkerchiefs, and other goods to small stores throughout the West.

In 1872, Strauss received a letter from Jacob Davis, a wholesale customer from Reno, Nevada. Davis, a Latvian-born tailor, fashioned clothing out of the fabric he purchased from Strauss. Davis had a customer who had commissioned him to make reinforced workpants, ones that would not split at the seams. Davis obliged, hammering copper rivets into the seams that were stressed during wear, including the corners of the pockets and the base of the fly.

Davis's riveted work pants were a resounding success. Word of mouth had their popularity soaring. Sensing a major business opportunity, and fearing imitators, Davis wrote to Levi Strauss. He wanted to patent the riveted pants but lacked the funds to pay the $68 (around $1,370 US in 2014) patent fee. If Strauss could pay the fee, Davis offered, they could produce the riveted workpants together. He assured Strauss that they would make a very large amount of money. On May 20, 1873, Strauss and Davis received US Patent No. 139,121 for their "Improvement in Fastening Pocket-Openings." This day is widely considered to be the birthday of blue jeans.

Designing the Solution

Although Jacob Davis may have technically invented riveted work pants, Levi Strauss's business acumen ensured their success. Strauss brought Davis to San Francisco to oversee the production of the first copper-riveted "waist overalls" (the original name for jeans). Originally, the pants came in two styles: one made from cotton duck, a heavy brown cloth, and another from a sturdy blue denim. Denim later became the standard. At first, the cloth was cut and sent to seamstresses who worked from home, but as demand grew, Strauss built factories throughout San Francisco.

A nineteenth-century advertisement for Levi Strauss & Co. clothing.

Applying the Solution

The heavy-duty, high-quality, durable construction made the pants perfect for miners and other hard laborers to wear to work. The riveted waist overalls revolutionized working clothes, becoming so popular that they came to be known simply as Levi's.

When the patent expired in 1891, dozens of imitators began making similar clothes. True Levi's could be identified by the now famous lot number "501," the double-arc stitching on the pockets, and the leather waistband patch bearing the two-horse logo. These details were all added to discourage **counterfeiting**. Each of these elements is still used.

Levi Strauss and Co. soon branched out into jackets, outerwear, and shirts. Toward the end of the nineteenth century, Strauss himself passed the day-to-day responsibilities to younger family members and turned his energies to other civic and business activities. Strauss was very active in San Francisco's Jewish community and was a member of San Francisco's first synagogue, Temple Emanu-El. As a longtime member of the San Francisco Board of Trade and as director of, variously, a bank, an insurance company, and the San Francisco Gas and Electric Company, he was also deeply engaged with the business community. His philanthropy was well known; in addition to funding more than two dozen scholarships at the University of California, Berkeley, Strauss contributed to many charities and local orphanages.

In 1902, Strauss died, leaving the bulk of the business to his nephews. He was remembered as one of San Francisco's leading citizens.

The Impact of the Solution on Society

The company headquarters and factories were destroyed during the devastating San Francisco earthquake in 1906. Levi Strauss and Co. rebuilt, and by the 1920s the company had become the leading brand of men's work wear in the western United States. In the 1930s and 1940s, with the popularity of early Westerns on movie screens, Levi's became a symbol of the American West, popularized by celebrities such as John Wayne, Gene Autry, and Gary Cooper. Levi Strauss and Co. capitalized on this imagery by advertising its "authentic cowboy pants." The pants were slowly becoming recognized more as leisure wear and less as work wear.

Levi's were introduced to Europe in the 1940s by soldiers stationed abroad during World War II. By the 1950s, the pants were sold in the Midwest and the East Coast for the first time. Postwar teenagers and young people began to wear Levi's, emulating the rebellious look and spirit of screen stars like Marlon Brando and James Dean.

By the 1960s, the original riveted-waist overalls had evolved into the jeans we know today. Belt loops were added in 1922, the zipper replaced the button-fly in 1955, and rivets disappeared from the back pockets in 1967.

Levi's enjoyed an even more stunning reputation abroad, particularly in the Soviet Union and in Communist Eastern Europe, where jeans became a highly coveted black market item in the 1980s. Indeed, the simple pair of denim pants came to represent American ideals of freedom, equality, and rugged individualism.

Amidst the modern deluge of denim brands, Levi's remain one of the most popular brands of jeans in the world. In 1994, *Fortune* magazine named Levi Strauss and Co. the most admired apparel company in the United States, not just for its jeans but also for its continuing spirit of philanthropy inspired by Levi Strauss. The company was an early leader in establishing AIDS support groups

The Great Jean Debate

Much debate swirls around the origins of the word "jeans." Some scholars say that "jean" comes from the word for a cotton fabric used to produce men's pants in Genoa, Italy, in the 1600s—"jean" being an English abbreviation of "Genoa."

By the end of the 1700s, two all-cotton fabrics were being produced in America, one called "denim" and the other called "jean." Denim (supposedly named after the city in France where it was first made: de Nîmes, meaning "of Nimes") was heavier and more durable. This is what Levi Strauss used for his riveted overalls in the late 1800s. Denim was a mix of white yarn and dyed yarn, usually an indigo color. Jean was produced with one color of thread and was not as rugged.

Jean cloth declined in popularity in the nineteenth century, just as denim grew in popularity because of Levi's. The word "jean" resurfaced in the 1950s and 1960s. It was adopted, first by the public and then officially by Levi Strauss and Co., as the accepted name for blue denim pants.

for employees (1983); in offering full medical care benefits to the unmarried partners of employees (1992); and in adopting worldwide standards for all its contractors regarding wages, hours, working conditions, and environmental responsibility (1993). In addition, Levi's are hailed as one of the few products to remain essentially the same since they were first produced.

Today the popularity of Levi's blue jeans continues. Across shopping malls, Levi's stores appear, and their unique branding makes them instantly recognizable. Examples of Levi's are even immortalized in the Smithsonian Institution in Washington, DC. Levi's jeans are testament to two men's idea and their determination to sell their idea to the world. Although Levi Strauss did not live to see just how influential his invention would become, his creation and his name live on.

Timeline

1829
Levi Strauss born as Loeb Strauss in Buttenheim, Germany

1847
Strauss moves to the United States

1850
Strauss changes his first name to Levi

1853
Strauss moves to San Francisco and founds Levi Strauss and Company

1872
Strauss receives a letter from Jacob Davis asking for help in obtaining a patent for his work pants

1873
Strauss and Davis receive a patent for their riveted work pants

1891
Strauss and Davis's patent expires

1902
Strauss dies

Earl Tupper

1907–1983

There have been many household goods that have improved the lives of people around the world. Perhaps one of the most significant was Tupperware, designed by Earl Tupper in the twentieth century. Tupper's invention changed the way people stored food. It continues to have an influence on food storage today. Moreover, the brand of storage containers Tupper created continues to be one of the most recognizable household brands in the world.

Starting Out

Earl Tupper was born on July 28, 1907, in Berlin, New Hampshire. His father was a farmer who also had a passion for inventing

Earl S. Tupper (*left*) and Brownie Wise (*right*) hold resin pellets at the Tupperware factory in 1951.

gadgets. Nothing much came of his tinkering, although he did receive a patent for a device used to clean chickens. To make ends meet, Tupper's mother, Lulu, operated a boardinghouse in the family's home and also took in laundry from neighbors for additional income.

While Earl Tupper was still a child, the family moved to Shirley, Massachusetts, and opened a greenhouse. From an early age, Earl had an obvious desire to succeed. When he was only ten years old, he began selling the family's produce door-to-door rather than at a farmers' market because he could sell much more. Upon graduation from high school in nearby Fitchburg in 1925, he continued to work in his family's greenhouse for a couple of years as well as at various odd jobs.

He also began taking correspondence courses (receiving class assignments and submitting results by mail), including one in advertising. Inspired by that course, he urged his family to undertake a more active marketing campaign for the greenhouse business. His enthusiasm for improving the family business was not shared by his parents, however, to Tupper's disappointment.

The Art of Inventing

Tupper began experimenting with various inventions at this time. He drew diagrams of his ideas in a notebook that he carried with him everywhere. These ideas ranged from the very modest, such as a type of comb that could be clipped to a belt, to the wildly impractical, such as his plan for a boat that would be powered by a large fish strapped to the bottom of its hull. He tried to promote his ideas to manufacturers but with no success.

Another of his correspondence courses had been in **tree surgery**, so around 1930 he began a company called Tupper Tree Doctors. He supported himself in landscaping and tree care for several years. In 1931, he married Marie Whitcomb. Together, the couple would have five children, the first of which was born a few years later. As the Depression became more severe for greater numbers of Americans, however, Tupper's client list shrank. Tupper Tree Doctors went bankrupt in 1936.

Defining the Problem

That failure helped spur Tupper to move in the direction of his true passion: inventing. He had determined as a boy that he would make a million dollars as an inventor by the time he was thirty years old. Although he missed that target by a few years, he was now more certain than ever that inventing was how he would achieve his ultimate success.

In 1937, Tupper met Bernard Doyle, founder of a plastics company in Leominster, Massachusetts. Leominster was becoming known as "plastic city," a manufacturing center where many pioneering inventors and entrepreneurs were establishing new concerns. Doyle's company, Viscoloid, had been bought by another company, DuPont, in 1928. Doyle brought Tupper into DuPont as a designer in 1937. At DuPont, Tupper later recalled, his true education began. Although he remained there for only one year, the time he spent there gave him valuable practical experience in design and manufacturing. It also introduced him to a wide range of contacts, who would be instrumental as Tupper set out on his own entrepreneurial ventures.

In 1938, Tupper left DuPont and founded the Earl S. Tupper Company. With some used molding machinery he had purchased, he began making small items such as beads and plastic cigarette

Women and Sales Force

The system of face-to-face marketing and sales that developed around Tupperware products was developed and refined mostly by women. That sales approach in turn opened important opportunities for women at a time when many other avenues remained closed to them.

During the years of American involvement in World War II, women entered the workforce in greater numbers because so many men were serving in the military. When soldiers returned home at the end of the war, they were given many of the jobs that women had held for the preceding years. The women were, in effect, sent back home.

Through its sales approach of holding home parties (Tupperware parties) designed to demonstrate and sell products directly to invitees, Tupperware provided millions of jobs to women. Mothers could schedule their parties and related sales activities around their other responsibilities. Typically, a Tupperware dealer would find other women willing to host events in their houses. These hostesses would invite their friends and family, and in return each hostess would receive a gift of a home product from the dealer. The Tupperware party became as popular a social phenomenon as Tupperware products were popular in the kitchen.

containers. Most of the work he did was as a **subcontractor** to DuPont. During World War II, Tupper's company prospered, largely because of its contracts to produce plastic moldings for gas masks as well as signal lamps for the military. After the war, Tupper refocused his efforts on his first and greatest interest: the civilian consumer market.

After developing a variety of products such as unbreakable drinking cups (for American Thermos), Tupper fixed his attention on creating a superior plastic container that would keep food fresh for an extended period. American consumers had not taken well to plastic containers in the past, partly because the plastic used had been of an inferior quality and, consequently, often peeled and made the food smell bad. Moreover, no plastic container had succeeded in maintaining freshness; air easily entered these containers and quickly spoiled the contents. Tupper set out to address both of these shortcomings.

It was not just as dealers of Tupperware that women could enjoy economic success. Those who wanted to branch out could do so by becoming managers of other dealers. Ambitious dealers would always be on the lookout for potential hostesses—and as they branched out, they might also look for other dealers to recruit. As managers, these women would train and motivate new recruits and earn a commission on the events they booked. Successful managers were eligible to become distributors, who were given exclusive rights to distribute Tupperware products in a given region of the country. However, a woman could become a distributor only on the condition that her husband join her in the enterprise, requiring that the husband quit his job. The financial opportunities for distributors during the 1950s and 1960s were such that couples usually accepted this condition. Still, the assumption that women could not fill the top positions in the hierarchy without their husbands' involvement speaks to the bias even within the very system that, in its era, was perhaps most favorable to women.

Designing the Solution

First, in 1938 he developed a superior type of plastic he called "Poly-T." (Tupper insisted throughout his life on the use of the word "Poly-T" instead of "plastic.") Poly-T was a variation of the polyethylene he had worked with at DuPont. Polyethylene—derived from **slag**—had been used during World War II as insulation for electrical wiring. A black, hard, foul-smelling substance, it was ill suited for domestic use. Tupper invented a method for refining and cleaning this slag to create a substance that was clear, lightweight, odorless, and hard yet flexible. The resultant Poly-T could bend without shattering, was resistant to heat, imparted no odors to food, and was very inexpensive.

Second, Tupper developed an improved Poly-T sealing lid for the container: his famous burping lid. This seal, based on the lip found on paint can lids, allowed the user to attach the lid to the plastic base, then, while gently pressing the middle of the lid, lift one edge off the lip slightly, thereby "burping," or expelling the air from the container before reattaching the lid over the container's grooved lip. Food kept inside this partial vacuum would stay fresh much longer. Now that he had perfected the composition and the design of his new product, all he needed was a way to show it to the wider public.

Applying the Solution

A true perfectionist, Tupper oversaw nearly every aspect of his production facility. He demanded the highest standards from everyone who worked for him, he designed every new style of Tupperware, and he looked over the shoulders of the people who ran his machines. Nevertheless, even though he was very driven to succeed, he was unable to bring his products to public attention at first. He initially marketed Tupperware by offering these items as "giveaways" with the purchase of some other product he was manufacturing, such as plastic cigarette cases for Camel. Finally, in 1946, he managed to introduce Tupperware into some hardware and department stores. What became known as the "Wonderbowl" gained wider attention and even won some design prizes. However, despite all the marketing efforts, the product was not selling very well, partly because of the bad reputation of previous plastics used for storing food. Both the quality of Tupper's plastic and the "Tupper seal" needed to be demonstrated to customers to create demand.

Soon after Tupperware began to appear on retail shelves, Stanley Home Products added it to a line of household products that the company demonstrated at parties held in private homes. Stanley's representatives did well with the product, selling Tupperware in homes much more effectively than it was being sold in retail stores. One agent in particular, Brownie Wise, had been selling Tupperware

Three women attending a Tupperware party in 1963

at a truly impressive rate from her office in Florida, where she purchased the product through local plastics distributors and resold it to the public. Tupper noticed and, in 1948, met with Wise and several other Stanley salespeople to discuss an overall marketing strategy for Tupperware. The salespeople persuaded Tupper that the home-demonstration party was the most effective way to market his product. Tupper adopted a plan based on Stanley's methods, and by 1950 Tupperware was enjoying wider distribution. In 1951, Tupper decided to discontinue supplying retail stores altogether and to rely solely on home-sales parties.

He established a new company, Tupper Home Parties, near Orlando, Florida, and appointed Wise to run it. The production headquarters remained in Massachusetts. In her first full year on the job, Wise managed to double Tupperware sales. The popularity of the home demonstration party, which would become universally known as the "Tupperware party," grew dramatically. After three years on the job, Wise had increased the number of Tupperware dealers from two hundred to more than nine thousand.

The Impact of the Solution on Society

Earl Tupper became increasingly estranged from the company he founded even as it enjoyed its greatest success. Correspondence between Wise and Tupper indicates that he had grown jealous of Wise for the prominent public role she had assumed as the face of Tupperware. In January 1958, Tupper fired Wise. Later that year, he sold the firm to the Rexall Drug Company for $16 million. Tupperware Home Parties continued to flourish under Rexall, with Tupper serving as chairman of the board of directors until 1973. That year, he moved with his family to Costa Rica, where he became a citizen and lived until his death of a heart attack on October 3, 1983. He was seventy-six years old.

Throughout the 1950s, Tupperware became more popular in American homes than any other kitchen product of its kind. Tupperware parties were held in millions of American households to introduce this new product to more consumers. By 1960, Tupperware parties were being held in Canada and Western Europe. Soon the phenomenon and the product were spreading across the globe. By the end of the twentieth century, Tupperware was facing competition from a wide variety of other plastic containers. Nonetheless, Tupperware can be found in nearly every country, with special products developed for particular culinary traditions, such as the "Kimchee Keeper" for sale in South Korea.

Tupper's invention changed the way people operated in the kitchen and stored their food. His strategy of selling directly to consumers has been a marketing tactic adopted by other companies and applied to many other products. Similarly, Brownie Wise's suggestion of hosting home parties has become a popular way for other companies and businesspeople to get their products known and purchased. However, this strategy has evolved with the digital age, and many home parties have moved from the household to the Internet. Today Tupper and his assistants' influence on the world of household food storage continues.

Timeline

1907
Earl Tupper born in Berlin, New Hampshire

1937
Tupper goes to work for DuPont

1938
Tupper founds the Earl S. Tupper Company; develops Poly-T plastic

1947
Tupper begins selling Tupperware

1948
Tupper meets Brownie Wise, a successful Tupperware home-sales agent

1951
Tupperware becomes available only through home-sales parties

1958
Tupper fires Wise

1973
Tupper retires

1983
Tupper dies

Glossary

atmospheric pressure The pressure exerted in every direction at any given point by the weight of the atmosphere.

biomimetics Biological mimicry, or the practice of using forms found in nature to inspire engineering or design.

bureaucracy A system of government or business run by a large group of people who are not elected.

centrifugal force The force that pushes things outward when they spin around in a circle.

conduit A pipe or tube through which something (such as water or wire) passes.

counterfeiting Copying a product, such as money, to make it look almost identical to the real product.

duct A pipe or tube for air, water, electric power lines, etc., to pass through.

durable Strong, sturdy; able to stay in good condition for a long time.

entrepreneur A person who aspires to become a successful businessperson and who may take risks with his or her products and money to do so.

Gulf Stream A warm current of water that flows north and west through the Atlantic Ocean off the East Coast of the United States.

nuclear fusion A way of generating energy by colliding small atoms so they join together.

photographic plate A piece of metal, called pewter, that is covered in a light-sensitive chemical, called bitumen, which is a kind of asphalt. It was used in early photo development.

prototype Test version of a product.

renege To go back on one's word.

robber baron A wealthy person who tries to get more money, land, or businesses in a wrong or dishonest way.

rote A way of learning by listening and repeating exactly what is said.

slag The waste product of refining crude oil.

subcontractor Someone who works for a set amount of time on a particular project.

supercooling Cooling water below its normal freezing point without turning it into ice.

tree surgery The act of cutting down trees.

Further Information

Introduction to Everyday Technology

Books   Bridgman, Roger. *1,000 Inventions and Discoveries*. New York: DK Publishing, 2014.

Challoner, Jack. *1001 Inventions That Changed the World*. Hauppauge, NY: Barron's Education, 2009.

Websites **How Static Electricity Works**
www.youtube.com/watch?v=fT_LmwnmVNM

Inventions that Shook the World: The 1900s
www.youtube.com/watch?v=JszhyeW73Q4

Nolan Bushnell: Pioneer of the Video Game Industry

Books   Bushnell, Nolan, and Gene Stone. *Finding the Next Steve Jobs: How to Find, Keep, and Nurture Talent*. New York: Simon & Schuster, 2013.

Frauenfelder, Mark. *The Computer: An Illustrated History from Its Origins to the Present Day*. London: Carlton Books, 2013.

Melissinos, Chris, and Patrick O'Rourke. *The Art of Video Games: From Pac-Man to Mass Effect*. New York: Welcome Books, 2012.

Websites **Atari Pong**
www.youtube.com/watch?v=e4VRgY3tkh0

BusinessWeek Interview with Nolan Bushnell
www.businessweek.com/articles/2014-12-04/atari-co-founder-nolan-bushnell-on-gamings-pioneer-years

Willis Carrier: Inventor of Air-Conditioning

Books   Basile, Salvatore. *Cool: How Air Conditioning Changed Everything*. New York: Fordham University Press, 2014.

Elridge, Alison, and Stephen Elridge. *The Coolest Inventor: Willis Haviland Carrier and His Air Conditioner*. Inventors at Work. New York: Enslow, 2014.

Websites **Carrier**
www.carrier.com

Who Made America?
www.pbs.org/wgbh/theymadeamerica/whomade/carrier_
hi.html

Josephine Cochran: Inventor of the Dishwasher

Books   Claybourne, Anna, and Adam Larkum. *The Story of Inventions.* 2nd ed. London: Usborne, 2012.

      Waisman, Charlotte S. *Her Story: A Timeline of the Women Who Changed America.* New York: Harper, 2008.

Website   **Lemelson-MIT Program: Josephine Cochrane**
lemelson.mit.edu/resources/josephine-cochrane

Louis Daguerre: Inventor of the Photograph

Books   Gustavson, Todd. *Camera: A History of Photography from Daguerreotype to Digital.* New York: Stirling Publishing, 2009.

      Parrish, Margaret, ed. *The Science Book.* New York: DK Publishing, 2014.

      Watson, Roger, and Helen Rappaport. *Capturing the Light: The Birth of Photography, a True Story of Genius and Rivalry.* New York: St. Martin's Press, 2013.

Websites   **Inventions of Photography: The Daguerreotype**
www.youtube.com/watch?v=d932Q6jYRg8

              A Thumbnail History of the Daguerreotype
daguerre.org/resource/history/history.html

George de Mestral: Inventor of VELCRO® Brand Fasteners

Books   Cutler, Nellie Gonzalez, ed. *The Big Book of How.* New York: Time, 2011.

      Gregory, Josh. *From Thistle Burrs to ... Velcro.* 21st Century Skills Innovation Library. North Mankato, MN: Cherry Lake Publishing, 2012.

Website   **How Does Velcro Work?**
www.youtube.com/watch?v=mgclivxODH0

Further Information

James Dyson: Inventor of the Cyclonic Vacuum Cleaner

Books   Dyson, James. *Against the Odds*. New York: Orion Books, 2003.

Gantz, Carroll. *The Vacuum Cleaner: A History*. Jefferson, NC: McFarland, 2012.

Website   **Dyson: A History of Invention**
www.youtube.com/watch?v=AMgeNjXtYx4

George Eastman: Inventor of the Handheld Camera

Books   Brayer, Elizabeth. *George Eastman: A Biography*. Rochester, NY: University of Rochester Press, 2012.

Coleman, A.D., Urs Stahel, and Joerg Bader. *Kodak City*. Berlin, Germany: Kehrer Verdlag, 2014.

Websites   **The George Eastman House**
www.eastmanhouse.org

Kodak: How George Eastman Revolutionized Photography
www.youtube.com/watch?v=cv2tOE4ioCl

Thomas Edison: Prolific Inventor

Books   Adkins, Jan. *Thomas Edison.* DK Biography. New York: DK Publishing, 2009.

Carlson, W. Bernard. *Tesla: Inventor of the Electrical Age*. Princeton, NJ: Princeton University Press, 2013.

DeGraaf, Leonard. *Edison and the Rise on Innovation*. New York: Stirling Publishing, 2013.

Websites   **The Inventions of Thomas Edison**
www.history.com/topics/inventions/thomas-edison

The True Story of Tesla and Edison
www.youtube.com/watch?v=KTIMWmRACxo

Daniel Fahrenheit:
Inventor of the Mercury Thermometer and Temperature Scale

Books   Chang, Hasok. *Inventing Temperature: Measurement and Scientific Progress*. New York: Oxford University Press, 2007.

Lin, Yoming S. *Fahrenheit, Celsius, and Their Temperature Scales*. Eureka! New York: PowerKids, 2011.

Websites   **Converting Fahrenheit to Celsius**
www.youtube.com/watch?v=C_YcfAvEo5o

How Stuff Works: Daniel Fahrenheit and the Mercury Thermometer
www.youtube.com/watch?v=kJm6gLiSehg

Philo Farnsworth: Inventor of the Electronic Television

Books   Castleman, Harry. *Watching TV: Six Decades of American Television.* 2nd ed. Syracuse, NY: Syracuse University Press, 2010.

Krull, Kathleen. *The Boy Who Invented TV: The Story of Philo Farnsworth*. New York: Dragonfly Books, 2014.

Websites   **The Most Famous Man You Never Heard Of**
www.youtube.com/watch?v=HHy04aN0jfl

Philo T. Farnsworth: Biography
www.biography.com/people/philo-t-farnsworth-40273

Benjamin Franklin: Prolific Inventor

Books   Franklin, Benjamin. *Poor Richard's Almanac*. Seattle, WA: Renaissance Classics, 2012.

Krensky, Stephen. *DK Biography: Benjamin Franklin*. New York: DK Publishing, 2007.

Websites   **Benjamin Franklin Sparks Electricity**
www.history.com/topics/american-revolution/benjamin-franklin/videos/ben-franklin-sparks-electricity

Science Show: Great Minds: Benjamin Franklin
www.youtube.com/match?v=Ki9mY6gMFpA

King C. Gillette: Inventor of the Disposable Safety Razor

Books   Schweikart, Larry. *American Entrepreneur: The Fascinating Stories of the People Who Defined Business in the United States*. New York: AMACOM, 2010.

Further Information

Waits, Robert K. *Before Gillette: The Quest for a Safe Razor*. Raleigh, NC: Lulu Enterprises, 2009.

Websites **Birth of an Icon: Gillette**
www.youtube.com/watch?v=j6wXBkeWlVg

Story of Gillette
money.cnn.com/magazines/fsb/fsb_archive/2003/04/01/341005/

Beulah Henry: Inventor of Household Devices

Book Magerison, Charles, Dr. *Amazing Entrepreneurs: Inspiring Stories*. Merseyside, England: Amazing People Club, 2010.

Website **IEEE – Beulah Louise Henry**
www.ieeeghn.org/wiki/index.php/Beulah_Louise_Henry

Walter Hunt: Inventor of the Safety Pin

Book Kane, Joseph Nathan. *Necessity's Child: The Story of Walter Hunt, America's Forgotten Inventor*. Charleston, SC: McFarland, 1997.

Websites **How Stuff Works: The World's Most Forgotten Inventor**
www.youtube.com/watch?v=u2La7s3Z5uE

Walter Hunt and the Safety Pin
inventors.about.com/od/hstartinventors/a/safety_pin.htm

Lonnie Johnson: Inventor of the Super Soaker

Book Walsh, Tim. *The Playmakers: Amazing Origins of Timeless Toys*. Sarasota, FL: Keys Publishing, 2004.

Website **Biography of Lonnie Johnson**
www.biography.com/people/lonnie-g-johnson-17112946#
early-life-and-education

Levi Strauss: Inventor of Levi's Blue Jeans

Books Downey, Lynn. *Levi Strauss & Co.* Images of America. Charleston, SC: Arcadia Publishing, 2007.

Johnston, Tony. *Levi Strauss Gets a Bright Idea: A Fairly Fabricated Story of a Pair of Pants*. New York: Houghton Mifflin Children's Books, 2011.

Websites   **How Stuff Works: The History of Blue Jeans**
www.youtube.com/watch?v=7pPbwNmo2pU

The Story of Levi's Jeans
www.levistrauss.com/our-story

Earl Tupper: Inventor of Tupperware

Books   Kealing, Bob. *Tupperware Unsealed: Brownie Wise, Earl Tupper, and the Home Party Pioneers*. Gainesville, FL: University of Florida Press, 2008.

Mason, Fergus. *Brownie Wise: Tupperware Queen*. Seattle, WA: LifeCaps, 2014.

Websites   **PBS: Earl Tupper**
www.pbs.org/wgbh/americanexperience/features/biography/tupperware-tupper

Tupperware
www.tupperware.com

Index

Index